Church of England, Diocese of Southwell, George Ridding

The Second Visitation Charge of George Ridding, D.D., Bishop of Southwell

to which are added some considerations on the Holy Communion, being

replies to questions asked in the diocese in the last four years

Church of England, Diocese of Southwell, George Ridding

The Second Visitation Charge of George Ridding, D.D., Bishop of Southwell
to which are added some considerations on the Holy Communion, being replies to
questions asked in the diocese in the last four years

ISBN/EAN: 9783337284848

Printed in Europe, USA, Canada, Australia, Japan

Cover: Foto ©Lupo / pixelio.de

More available books at **www.hansebooks.com**

THE SECOND

VISITATION CHARGE

OF

GEORGE RIDDING, D.D.,

BISHOP OF SOUTHWELL.

TO WHICH ARE ADDED

SOME CONSIDERATIONS ON

THE HOLY COMMUNION,

BEING REPLIES TO

QUESTIONS ASKED IN THE DIOCESE

IN THE LAST FOUR YEARS.

1893.

London : Simpkin, Marshall, Hamilton, Kent & Co., Limited.

Nottingham : C. J. Sisson, S.P.C.K. Depôt, Albert Street.

Derby : Miss E. Mee, S.P C.K. Depôt, The Strand.

Southwell : John Whittingham, Queen Street.

PRICE ONE SHILLING.

age 10, line 34, for 'make' read 'makes'

,, 12, line 7, for 'reparation' read 'separation'

,, 27, line 32, for 'hearts,' read hearts'

,, 49, for 'Cacilius' read Cæcilius'

,, 50, lines 12, 15, 18, for '*profesti*' read '*nefasti*'

I.

My Dear Brethren,

My Visitations during 1892 have given me a series
of interesting meetings through the Deaneries. I have tried
several different forms of Conference, but I have concluded
that the best is the most established form, viz., that of a
Service and Address in Church and a Conference of Clergy
and Laity afterwards, with, if wished for special reasons, a
Chapter of Clergy as well. Shorter days seemed to fail in
substantial. effectiveness. For the purposes of Conference
groups of several Deaneries together have been in most districts preferred to single Deaneries; but, efficient as some of
the grouped meetings have been, they scarcely reach or
express the local lay feeling so well as meetings nearer home.
However, Deaneries have their own characteristics, and in
all meetings success really means preparation. I cannot
attend every Deanery Conference in one year, but I hope, if
it please God, to distribute visits to them. I hope the
Conferences will not be barren, and that not only ideas have
been suggested, but that their Resolutions will be carried
out This year the Deaneries of Chesterfield, Dronfield
and Staveley led the way in voting support to the Schools'
Sustentation Fund, and were followed by five Deaneries at
Southwell, three at Bakewell, and by Repton. I hope the
support will come. Repton agreed also with the Chesterfield
Conference in desiring The Young Man's Friendly Society
to be started in their Deaneries; and with Bakewell about
Schools' Benefit Clubs. A Deanery seems just the Unit for
these Organizations, as for some others, e.g. for Associations
of Lay Helpers, which Bakewell and Alfreton have voted to
start ; and Associations for instructing Pupil Teachers
were discussed by six Deaneries at Derby, but need wider
and more real consideration than they have received. For
Technical Classes, too, as Ashburne, Repton, South and
West Bingham voted, Ruridecanal districts seem to suggest
Units to the County Councils. I shall rejoice to hear of
these good ideas being realized.

A

As I have 'repeated,' these occasions of co-operating supply antidotes to Rural Clergy Isolation. First years must not discourage. I observe that in its third year the Southwell Ruridecanal Church Restoration Society reports eleven out of seventeen parishes as contributing Church Collections, and assisting substantially three of the four Churches requiring it, with premonitions of helping the fourth if it will be helped. I welcome this example from the Cathedral Deanery, as I welcome also the evidence in the returns to the attention paid in that Deanery to the suggestions made at my last Visitation. The changes reported generally are not many. 35 more Churches are insured, but over 100 are still not insured. 15 more Terriers are added, but over 150 parishes are still without. 14 Schools have been given up, making more than one fifth of the parishes without schools : though this fifth includes a certain number of small linked parishes in the country, as well as new districts in large towns. Meanwhile, the list of Churches in ruins has almost disappeared. I do not mean that no Churches have weak points noticed in the Visitation returns. About 30 in Derbyshire are returned as wanting something done to tower or walls or roof, to satisfy complete inspection. But now that Taddington is recovered, Egginton well restored, and S. Peter's, Derby, and Chapel-en-le-Frith, are taken in hand, the list of discreditable blots named in my last charge is cleared off. The noble promise of the new Church of S. Werburgh's Derby, and the unusually fine restoration of Spondon, have elevated two of the poorest into two of the finest Churches of the county. Ashburne has been saved from disaster : Bradley is made quite passable, and I hope that East Sterndale is in course of amendment. I regret the delay in the proposed enlargement of Killamarsh. Norbury and Pinxton alone "make no sign." In Notts, though more has been done, there is also more still undone. A beautiful new Memorial Church has taken the place of its finest ruin at Colston Bassett. Close by, another Memorial Church at Aslockton makes a model village example. Wilford, Beckingham, Saundby, Carlton in Lindrick, have been restituted with admirable effect. The most startling disfigurement has been removed in the Chancel at Rampton. The two worst ruins promised to be fully restored this year at Egmanton, and Woodborough, and are nearly completed. The first instalment of Willoughby is done, and Edingley is begun. Farndon was taken just in time, and will be a striking work. The little Church at Sookholms is the latest addition to this list of really needed revivals during this year.

During the four years since my last Visitation, Churches have been built, or so much enlarged as to need Consecration, at Old Radford, Ruddington, Clumber, Selston Underwood, Colston Bassett, and Aslockton, Brampton S. Thomas, Carlton in Willows, Hyson Green, Wilford, and S. George's Nottingham.

Substantial Restorations of Churches have been made at Sawley, Tibshelf, Normanton on Soar, Codnor, Bunny, S. Collingham, Fledborough, Orston, Rolleston, Castleton, Laneham, Trowell, Ratcliffe-on-Soar, Egginton, Carlton-in-Lindrick, Rampton, Beckingham, S. Alkmund's Derby, Ashburne, Spondon, Taddington, Saundby, Willoughby, and in the little churches of Cotham, Cottam, Stanton on the Wolds, and Sookholms, as well as effective renovations in Foremark, Ossington, Donisthorpe, Ashford, Flawborough, Hazlewood and Shottle, besides minor improvements in a number of other parishes.

Eighteen substantial Mission churches have been opened: at S. Dunstan's Derby, Bolsover, Marlpool, Borrowash, Barnby Moor, Holbech, Rainworth, Belper Openwood Gate, Belper Lane End, Boulton, N. Wingfield, Staveley, Speedwell, Pleasley Hill, S. Margaret's Nottingham, Ambergate, Cossall, S. Mark's Mansfield, Hucknall Torkard; besides useful additions, in some cases of special interest, at Brampton, Killamarsh, Ironville, Mugginton, Alfreton, Hackenthorpe, Unstone, Etwall, and S. Mary's Ilkeston.

Seventy parishes, or one seventh of the Diocese, have during these four years received improvements in their church buildings. In my last charge I spoke of 60 others, and said that, if the same rate was maintained till this time, the Diocese would have nearly made good its defects. The rate has been more than maintained: still, even when the good and important works already named as in hand are completed, and without mentioning the repairs desired in official inspections at a number of places, I cannot honestly exclude from a list of notables any of the following : Bothamsall, Elton, Gringley, Langford, S. Leverton, Maplebeck, N. Muskham ; the small linked churches of Austerfield, Stokeham, Syerston, and the remaining stages of Orston, Rampton, Rolleston, and Willoughby.

The church accommodation holds generally a fair proportion to the population. In many villages the whole population could go to church together. In whole Deaneries such as Ashburne, S. Bingham, E. Newark, Tuxford, there are two seats to three persons : in Derby, one to six, Nottingham one to seven, in Mansfield Deanery one to eight. But these aggregates leave it possible for Old Radford and Hyson Green, and S. Peter's, Derby, to have only one to fourteen ; S. Luke's, Derby, and Sutton in Ashfield one to twelve; Church Gresley, and nothwithstanding several efforts to increase, Hucknall Torkard, and the Nottingham districts of S. Ann's and the Meadows still one to ten. On the other side I cannot forbear to set Staveley providing one to four-and-a-half by six Mission chapels, Chapel-en-le-Frith and Tideswell by five Mission chapels for one to two-and-a-half. In some of the cases selected above, there have been past difficulties to account for the backward position, which have passed away, leaving brighter prospects possible : in some greater efforts are being made. But I am obliged to admit that progress at Nottingham, in the completion of 'prospected' churches and districts, has during these four years been very discouraging to the Clergy in charge of forming the new districts, who find it beyond their powers to collect money to build the churches necessary for the formation of the districts, of which five have been for some years struggling in half-formed existence. In the rest of the Diocese the problem is not to provide for numbers so much as to reach the scattered items. In some cases I had hoped ere this to see districts separated, e.g., Fernilee, 12 miles from its mother church, Bugsworth 9 miles off, Whaley Thorns five miles, Holloway as far : all substantial places, but requiring to be separated before they can obtain permanent settlement. Where distances are less, there is so much to be said for keeping a large parish in the country together round one Parish Church, with ministrations in circuit through its hamlets, that I should not wish to break districts off hastily. But such a parish as e.g. Tideswell is endowed as a whole above the standard for receiving help from public funds, and yet certainly not enough to keep a staff of several Curates ; nor have such country parishes resources in themselves to maintain Curates. On the other hand, if districts are made, public contributions for Curates are withdrawn. So we are on the horns of a dilemma. The question of provision for our hamlets has been threshed out in so many conferences, that we know the alternative possibilities (or impossibilities) ; 1 Lay ministrations in single hamlets or in circuit ; 2 More parish Curates ; 3 Assistant Clergy to visit circuits of hamlets in several neighbouring parishes ; 4 Fresh subdivision of parishes. The conclusion generally reached is that the increase of parish Curates, aided by brave use of Lay ministers, is a more reliable solution than mixing or multiplying parishes. Money is of course required for that, but only money, and that not in the lump sums needed for permanent endowment, but only in the measure to supply needs while felt and services while valued. Still, money is needed, and valuable as is the help of A.C.S. in the populous districts of this Diocese, neither it nor the Ecclesiastical Commissioners touch the widespreading but sparsely inhabited hill districts, where the distances and number of hamlets baffle a clergyman's powers even more than large populations in small areas. What is wanted is more endowment given specially for Curates or Lay Helpers and only paid for them.

In saying this, I must be understood not to be speaking of the entirely distinct subject of the poverty of many livings. In Derbyshire, putting aside 10 villages which are not joined to other parishes, but are allowed to be held with others, there are 10 parishes held alone which have not £100 a year, Chaddesden, Elmton, Kniveton, Long Lane, Lullington, Measham, Scropton, Stanley, Tissington, Turnditch, Willington, of which most are no doubt small, but Elmton, Stanley, Measham, and Willington are substantial places, and the first two require two places of worship. Thirty parishes held alone have under £150, among which Bolsover and Wirksworth are two specially heavy charges ;

Barrow and Bradborne have two churches each ; Brassington, Dore, Pentrich, Pilsley, Repton, are too large for such stipend ; Chellaston, Chelmorton, Hognaston, Holmesfield, King Sterndale, South Darley, are only recently raised above £100 ; besides which are Atlow, Barlow, Littleover, two Osmastons, Elton, Mapperley, Wilford, Quarndon, Rosliston, Thorpe, Trusley, Wessington—some have fallen below £150 from the reduction of values, but that is not the usual case. There are also 26 parishes of between £150 and £200—in all, 77 parishes in Derbyshire out of 251 are of less income than £200.

In Nottinghamshire 26 livings are between £150 and £200 ; 10 are between £100 and £150, Egmanton, Elkesley, Flintham, Gamston and Eaton, Hayton, Langford, Langar, Scofton, Whatton, and Willoughby. The 10 are all cases which ought to be augmented. There are 16 below £100, Annesley, Bothamsall, Cotham, Edwalton, Elton, Kneeton, Kilvington, Maplebeck, Ossington, Owthorpe, Ratcliffe, Sibthorpe, Stanton, Tithby, Wellow, Winkburn : of these, however, only Annesley, Bothamsall, Edwalton, Tithby, and Wellow are held alone. In all, out of 236 livings in Nottinghamshire, 52 are below £200. The practice of uniting two, and often three, villages in one benefice has been followed to a much greater extent in Notts than in Derbyshire. Reductions from the fall of values have been also more widespread and more severe in Notts. Langar, Kilvington, and Gamston are examples of livings fallen within a few years to one fourth, one fifth, and one seventh of their old values. Of the 27 livings in the Diocese below £100 a year, only one is in public patronage, Stanley, which is, from growth and circumstances, the most pressing case for being augmented. Of the 42 under £150, nine in Derbyshire and three in Notts are in public patronage. Of the 42 under £200, five in Derbyshire and eight in Notts. are in public patronage. To raise these 26 livings in public patronage to £200 a year would require £50,000. To raise all the 130 livings which are below £200 a year to that amount would require not much less than £300,000. A certain number have till lately been above £200 : in others the population is so small that it cannot claim such provision, and the choice must be between uniting parishes together and finding men who prefer the small charge and the small income. In others the best supplement is made by the ancient custom of Easter offerings in recognition of faithful service. There are other parishes, in which the patrons make the ideal solution by themselves augmenting the benefices up to £200 : I wish I had information complete enough to make a list of them ; but these are returned as of that value and not reckoned in the list above. Where livings have fallen, as in E. and S. Notts more particularly, it has been due to depression, felt equally by the landowners and farmers, who are disabled from supplementing losses which they share. Common suffering may promote sympathy, but cannot exempt one class. It should be one advantage of the wider area of a Diocese, in which prosperity may be attending one part or one kind of property, while others are in adversity, that some common stock or fund might be maintained by which suffering places might be recovered. Our Poor Benefice Funds exist for that purpose. But they are too feeble to do much. In Derbyshire a generous gift of Mr. Strutt's some years ago has practically been the society's fund since I have been here, and out of it a number of benefices have been helped to acquire substantial improvements : but that fund is exhausted. The Notts Fund has been still less capable of effective augmentation. While church restorations have been generously aided, mainly in response to laborious exertions of the clergy, aid to augment clergy incomes is not so urgently asked by the clergy, nor does it attract generally a ready response. I am ashamed at saying this. For my only appeal of the kind made for our Peak District at Buxton met so generous a response from so many, especially in the Duke of Rutland's exemplary bestowal of the Rectorial Tithes on two parishes, that it might well have made me a beggar. As indeed I gratefully acknowledge that I have been always encouraged by kind response to the occasional personal appeals that I have made. But I believe that beggars are, like poets, born—not made. I almost despair of being made one. Still I can try. I want £100,000 to make our starvings into livings. Are there not 10 men worth £10,000 ? Who will begin ?

Does this sound mockery or levity? It is not so meant. But there may be unreasonableness on one side as well as the other. It is wild talk to claim, when tithes sink, that one generation should redress the balance and raise all livings to an adequate standard : still more to call on Bishops to induce this, on pain of censure for heartlessness. The clergy have not generally joined in such wild talk which they know to be untrue and unworthy of their order. If here or there, extreme hardships have driven one man or another to urge their necessities too importunately, people who are vexed may more justly reflect how such exceptions manifest the rule of uncomplaining silence, such as has so markedly met depressions in other classes also. This depression is however what has wrung the present cry. Comfortable people may well be asked to think how little margin for retrenchments is allowed by these falling stipends, when the assigned house must still be kept up and when parish duties and usefulness necessitate servants. Parish efficiency must needs suffer. 'The tale of bricks cannot be made without straw.' There is much occasion for considerate supplementings of these depressed incomes, and where faithful ministry has been valued, I trust it will meet recognition in such wise considerateness from those more fortunate. The clergy would not wish me to say more of this. It is quite a distinct subject from what seems to be mixed up with it, the existence of extremely poor livings, of which I was speaking. Of these, I cannot help repeating that a number are not posts to claim a larger income, if compared with other posts of like importance. If too large houses have been built on them, we now begin to regret that it was lately thought that large houses redeemed small incomes. Our present clergy do not feel it so. We may perhaps regret, too, that some villages were separated, instead of being worked with curates from the central mother parish. But curates are rarely planted out to live in hamlets, and it is men's living there that make their influence. Curates too, however they talk, when old enough for sole charge, if not before, prefer 'a poor thing, but mine own.' But having courted 'the poor thing' portionless, it is more natural than reasonable to claim afterwards a portion which others might have courted. However curates are wise who press for augmentation of livings. What they want is a future. As curates for ten years they are better off than curates ever were, and than most professions' beginnings. What clergy in common with all large departments or services, should desire as the finance arrangements to give strength, is work for the young, good pay for middle age, and better retirement for the old. The age has gone on a wrong tack in swamping pensions to pay work. But as the means of augmentation, let them desire, in the interest of all alike, that having secured endowment enough to make men independent for teaching, they should, like other teachers, for what is more, rest on the satisfaction of their people. The true augmentation is the yearly offerings of the people. Our Prayerbook still directs people at Easter to reckon their duty to the minister, and in that rule provides the wisest form of supplemental endowment. Patrons and wealthy churchmen should revive this Easter duty, as some do generously, and consider what faithful clergy are in any ministerial relation to them, which may claim from them as due for faithful service substantial gifts proportioned to their wealth, whereby they should escape living on ancestral benefactions and bear their natural living part in maintaining Christ's Church. There is more wealth now then when benefactions endowed churches, and its possessors are doubtless pressed for doles with endless importunities. But, after all, these importunities abound because that wealth does not, instead of doles, endow upon the scale of the olden time. I pray that those who do this already, will not think that I speak of them, but those who don't. But is there nothing done? do churchpeople give nothing? is there no ministry maintained by voluntary gifts? Scarcely a curate in this Diocese is not so maintained, by people's offerings to meet Grants from Ecclesiastical Commission, or A.C.S., or our own Church Extension Societies, and by the wider subscriptions to those Societies. If curates are better paid than when I was young, most incumbents are relieved from paying them, as when I was young. No Societies are greater help to the church and clergy : it is easily forgotten, how new that help is. No doubt they mean more ministers, not richer ones. Can they be richer too? That brings me back again. Are there not men who would scorn the thought that they would be impoverished if some accident lost them £3000 a year? Once gone, they would not feel it. Men have given it for one building, and for lodging houses. So one man might make livings out of all the starvings of the Diocese.

Since my last charge one Buxton meeting raised a Fund for the poor livings in the Peak district of Derbyshire, with which seven livings were augmented substantially ; Taddington and Monyash by the Duke of Rutland, Earl Sterndale by the Duke of Devonshire, up to the standard usually named : Chelmorton, Rowsley, King Sterndale, by subscriptions and grants fairly towards it : S. Darley and Matlock Bank another stage onwards :

B

and five others have some useful benefaction ready when they can avail themselves of it. The poverty of the whole district was exceptionally general, and commanded an attention, for which I am most grateful. But it was also exceptionally an example how such poor districts come to exist. Subdivisions of vast parishes, notably of Bakewell, they were formed with the legal minimum pittance for reparation, and left to struggle by stages to reach competence if they could. Such places require saintliness, and try it sore. I rejoice with thankfulness that that district has been so far improved. No other was quite like it in uniform poverty, and I have not felt any other similar opening for a local appeal. For the rest an appeal must be more general for the Diocese.

It has been gratifying in these four years to find the support of the Derbyshire Church Extention Society renewed for the second Quinquennium of the new Diocese with considerable increase over the first. We have to thank the Duke of Devonshire for his able advocacy of it. The Society has been again enabled to contribute towards improvements of some livings in the houses and stipends, without reducing the Mission curates. But this could not practically be made the society's main work without crippling its chief established use in providing those curates. In Notts, no such Archidiaconal Society exists, and the Spiritual Aid Society of Nottingham, gallantly as its officers struggle for it, is scarcely enabled to maintain its large engagements, and quite unable to take a fresh branch. The natural organisation for the augmentation of poor livings exists in each Archdeaconry in their Poor Benefice Funds, and my best wish on this important subject is, that those who are not personally in a position to make direct augmentation of livings, may make their contributions to those two Poor Benefice Funds.

I have desired in my agricultural deaneries to collect advice about the hours for Sunday services most suitable for those engaged with cattle and dairy work, and more particularly for the requirements of the latterly developed milk trade, dependent on train service hours. It is clearly difficult to meet the exigencies of the Sunday labor, unavoidable in the case of cattle, and we must obey the cows. But I found a very general agreement that an early afternoon service would be the best arrangement. It might even be well to invert the common plan by having children's service and catechising in the morning, and making the afternoon the principal village service. With the help of the moon, monthly (or bi-monthly) evening services might be added of, perhaps, a more ' mission ' character, which might suit some of the lads best. I hope I shall be pardoned if I say that it has occurred to me to wonder if at such services a course from some interesting, good book might not alternate effectively with sermons of affectionate and straight advice, based on personal acquaintance. At such services, too, the most inhuman theorist would subordinate music to hymns, which should make the singing Congregational. Men of the Diocese constantly appeal to me for such hymns in my travels. I delight in the devoted choirs which I find through the Diocese, and I enter into anthems being sung on occasions with a big O, but I sympathize also with the popular taste for tunes which are tunes. After all said and done, however, I suspect that our cow and milk boys must be coaxed into personal friendship like other young men, and that it will be in the parsonage and by pleasant ways that they will be drawn to feel pastoral influence, when, and as, they can be caught. Knowledge of other young male Britons prevents my despairing of boys, who are imperfect church attendants in hobbledehoyhood, growing into religious fathers of families: but how happily, and in what Christian body, their manhood develops its religion, will often depend on the degree of care and friendliness which they remember to have received personally from their clergyman as boys.

I rejoice to repeat what I said four years ago, of the satisfaction I find in the careful and well ordered services which are general in our churches, in the reverent ministrations, in the large and effective choirs, in the care taken generally of the churches, and the full and attentive congregations. I also lament still, as I did then, that I so rarely hear any of the Clergy preach. I have little to say of changes in these respects, and even when some changes of incumbents may have been expected to revolutionize the existing use, I have observed, not without satisfaction, a reasonable maintenance of continuity, and that there has been concurrence, if not initiation, on the part of the people in changes when made.

Thirty-five more churches have weekly communions since

1888 ; making up about two fifths of the parishes. The numbers confirmed have not increased since 1888, which recorded the highest total reached in any year. I hoped that the appointment of a Suffragan Bishop and a consequent multiplication of centres would have enabled us to have had a better proportion to our population. The last census made our population close upon a million. But our confirmations were not quite 6750. I have wished to hold confirmations in every church, and this wish has been accepted in the deaneries. But it has, perhaps, acted unhappily in two ways. Not only have small places not attracted bigger neighbours, but the idea has spread, and been, perhaps, encouraged, that candidates should delay till another turn should come for their own church. I repeat my strong deprecation of this. Not only are many thereby left out altogether, but for most it loses their best opportunity, and it weakens the preparation, possible for small yearly classes, by swamping them in masses at intervals. I am glad to believe that it is due to higher estimation of the rite and its obligations more than to neglect or opposition, that candidates have not increased. I rejoice more and more at the apparent reality of those who come. But you will have seen that I have thought the time come to remind people that confirmation is meant to be a help to the weak and imperfect, and not a sign of perfection. I am unchanged in my opinion that, for our ordinary young people individually, the age of greatest reality and help in confirmation is not younger than 15 or 16 ; but in some special cases where I have felt that a clergyman has kept his school close to him in fatherly touch as the natural confirmation class, this has presented a particular and true corporate form of spiritual preparation of the generation. The general advance of school education at any rate makes a younger age reasonable for acceptance in point of intelligence, and I quite sympathize with the fatherly anxiety ' to be in time ' for character.

The mention of the Bishop Suffragan has reminded me that, what has become so integral a fact of the Diocese, has only been established since my last charge. It has been a source of unfailing joy to me to find how welcome his presence has been in every place visited by him, and how deeply and truly his Christian wisdom, singlemindedness, and sympathy have been appreciated, and nowhere more than in his own town and seat of Derby.

Once more I must repeat, as I cannot fail to do in this charge, the expression of our common lament, both public and private, for the loss of so special a leader in the Diocese as Archdeacon Balston, and with that must join the expression of happy relief that we have been spared the loss, which seemed nearly imminent, of the Archdeacon of Nottingham, now happily restored to his energetic duty, in which he has a most able and willing yokefellow in the new Archdeacon of Derby. In my last charge I had to speak of our Rural Deaneries as scarcely completed. Of the 31 deans then just commissioned, 12 have since ceased to hold office (three in Notts. and nine in Derbyshire), four only from death, eight from health or removal into other deaneries. *Uno avulso, non deficit alter Aureus.* But while thanking, with the gratitude of anticipation, their successors, I look back with special regret on the loss of some of my first selection. Visitation returns emphasize nothing more clearly than the ways in which Rural Deans may make their special mark in their deaneries. The office becomes more and more the pivot of diocesan work, and I feel more and more the dependence of diocesan progress on the Rural Dean's centripetal influence on his deanery towards Diocesan ideas and co-operation.

Since my last charge, many important organizations, then foreshadowed, have been established, and made genuine and satisfactory progress to a degree easily overlooked, and to which I feel it therefore well to advert.

The Society of Mission Clergy was founded in Nov., 1888, and has been actively at work during these four years, its members having conducted 40 missions in the Diocese, and 30 outside of it, 60 Quiet Days, and 65 courses of sermons and instructions. Some fear seems still to survive lest parish missions mean sensationalism, and there are districts which have not adopted them. I am able to answer for the sobriety of our missioners' methods, and though missions cannot be a substitute for pastoral efficiency, I believe that pastoral efficiency will find in them a valuable periodic instrument for realising and deepening spiritual life. The clergy will desire

me to take this opportunity of referring with special gratitude
and satisfaction to the Diocesan Clergy Retreat, conducted last
year so ably by Canon Arthur Mason, at Repton School, with
so much assistance from the unique fitness of the place as well
as the completeness of all arrangements made there for the
clergy by the head and assistant masters, to whom all
present, but none more than myself, have desired to record
our most grateful appreciation. Canon Keymer has been an
invaluable secretary to the society.

More recently, but with as full promise of developing its
help, the Church Reading Society has in the last three years
given lectures on the Bible, Prayer Book, and Church History, to classes of considerable size at Derby and Nottingham
and seven other important centres, with between 600 and
700 members. In six centres permanent Libraries have been
established. More lecturers are wanted : this work having
been done, with valued outside help from Canons Crowfoot
and Lonsdale, by nine men, Archdeacon Freer and Mr. Sing
bearing the main brunt. It is in contemplation that the
Diocese should join two or three of its neighbours to form a
district for an S.P.C.K. lecturer on Doctrine and Church
History, who will, it is hoped, co-operate with the Church
Reading Society.

My last charge forecast the formation of a Woman's
League for Mothers and Women in positions of Responsibility, to unite the different departments of women's religious
and philanthrophic work, and to assist each place to start
without isolation the organizations specially suited to it.
This Women's League has in these four years established 81
branches round eight other chief centres, with about 4000
members, and promises to be a most valuable instrument.

In 1889 the Diocese adopted the agency of a Fair Mission
Woman, and her special fitness, zeal and prudence, under
wise direction and with cordial co-operation from magistrates
and police, has been instrumental in promoting welcome im-
provement in the shows and conduct of the Fairs, and their
consequent better enjoyment.

Besides these moral agencies, the Diocesan Finance Association has been created since 1888, to be a Body capable of
holding Trusts, especially for buildings of mixed use, such

as mission chapels used also for school or parish purposes, for which there has been hitherto no legitimate form of corpor·ate Trustees. The Association has been at once found useful for a number of that class of buildings, and will be available to hold houses or monies in temporary Trusts Our Diocesan societies being managed by unpaid officers, there is no reason to expect or desire their funds to be transferred to the Association, as in some other Dioceses, but as a Diocesan Trust agency it supplies a much felt need.

These are all fresh Diocesan agencies since my last charge. With them the older agencies have generally shown active development. The Ladies' Home Mission Association in aid of the A.C.S , which in 1888 was scarcely known in Notts., has branches now in all the Deaneries of the Diocese, and has· more than trebled its contributions. The Girls' Friendly Society has enlarged its borders by 40 parishes and 1000 members, and its departments are full of life. There has been considerable progress in the Diocesan Rescue and Preventive Work, which is not only active at its chief centres of Derby and Nottingham, but has now also been spread to several of the other chief towns. I could wish that there was more recognition and support given in the Diocese to the Diocesan Penitentiary Fund, on which such Rescue Work ought to be able to rest.

My Visitation returns shew a very general parochial activity in promoting institutes, temperance societies and bands of hope, penny banks, cricket and football clubs, bands and music clubs, and in the large towns recreation rooms and lads' brigades. Such things are of course not the pastors' most completely spiritual opportunities, nor have small villages the same use for them if the clergyman knows all his people as a family. But they are in themselves social links for the people, which may also form friendly links with the clergyman, and I believe very much in the mutual advantages of these societies.

The public church questions of the year 1892 have been the Clergy Discipline Act, the agitation for Church Disestablishment in Wales, the working of the Free Education Act, and the termination of the protracted law suit of Read and Others v. Bishop of Lincoln.

Of the Clergy Discipline Act I spoke so fully in my last charge in 1888, that the small alterations made this year in the former Draft Bill seem to need no special remarks. The Act is one originated by Convocation, and fully deliberated for several years. It had reached that position when it was taken into Parliament, and passed according to Parliamentary opportunities. Those cannot be regulated for Convocation, and no sane man can complain of the procedure followed, except so far as the Four Houses of Convocation found it beyond them to act as one. The power of Deprivation has been judged to be a proper ultimate resource : I believe that its action will be preventive and not penal, and I trust it will prove preventive enough.

What exaggerations of the need of such an Act may become current was lately exemplified in the publication in the *Pall Mall* of a letter purporting to give a list of criminous clergy gathered by the writer from a year's newspapers. Enquiry proved that the letter was fictitious. I have been able to ascertain that it was due to the change of editors and staff taking place on the very day, that no explanation of the hoax has been made by the *Pall Mall.* But meanwhile a number of other newspapers copied and commented on the list, and currency was given to an unwarrantable fabrication, which has not been withdrawn.

Of the agitation for Disestablishment of the Church in Wales, our Diocese has repeatedly affirmed in every possible way its opinion that the Welsh Dioceses are no separate Church from the English, and that all must stand together. I shall not say more of it. But in regard to the general question, I desire to present to churchmen, who are restive about Church Legislation, and think churchmen would provide endowments, and, if they won't, are ready to fly to the moon—my belief, in which, perhaps, I stand alone, that Disestablishment would alter the Church's power for good as much as Disendowment. It means the destruction of the parochial system, which has been the Church's real influence. The clergy derive from their legal position the three things which they value most : Their freehold tenure, their freedom from clergy intrusion, their authority to pastor their whole parish. Laymen may fret at times under the first two privileges, till they contrast them with Nonconformist ministers' dependence, and their rival subdivisions after disputes. But for the clergy the change would mean still more the loss of the authority which justifies their visiting their parish not as volunteer philanthropic intruders but as national officers appointed for this very thing and regarded as such. The unrivalled acquaintance with the poor and power to direct help for them, which the clergy are recognized to possess in East London, is in many cases independent of endowment, where men are maintained from voluntary resources, and might continue the same if the Church were disendowed ; but it rests on their position as parsons of the parishes, which causes a claim and forms an introduction which would be destroyed by Disestablishment. Nonconformist ministers cannot do the same, if they would : but Disestablishment would neither make them able nor willing. The parson's position would not be divided but destroyed. What advantage to the people this would be, what liberty or enlightenment or comfort or help any but Secularists can see in this, is as puzzling as it is to say, what benefit it is to children to debar them from the acquaintance and interest of the clergyman, who is to most of them just the influence not supplied by their own surroundings. Look at a workhouse, where a chaplain is extruded, and ministers of all denominations are invited to divide the office among them. It may gratify the ministers at first, but what of the poor ? Can all those ministers befriend any one poor person effectively by turns, or can any poor person know and value all the ministers by turns ? If a man tells me that 20 20ths of a man must make a man, I ask him to break himself into 20 pieces and try. Such workhouse crises shew one side of the question as East London shews the other. If chaplains are extruded in spite of Acts and Local Government Board, one Christian undenominational layman attached for moral and religious supervision of inmates and staff alike could serve the country's purpose better than the ministers of all the sects bowing each other in and out and taking a service each once a quarter. Only such a lay officer would cost more than guardians pay chaplains, and he must not be dismissable by the guardians. What spiritual provision would be made for the out-poor by parish boards like guardians may be inferred from what guardians make for the in-poor. The rates might be saved, but would the souls? It is all askew to make Church Establishment a question of equality between competing bodies. It is a question of having appointed officers to do a particular great national work that won't be done without. However, I am addressing churchmen, and return to my first words, that if churchmen suppose that the position of a National Church may be lightly surrendered, they have not in my judgment realized the difference in religious influence belonging to congregational and parochial systems. For the clergy it might be easier work (and in our large towns we may see how readily clergy may drop into such a system), if their attention became limited to their congregation, over whom, too, some ecclesiastically minded clergy may (vainly) expect to exercise discipline : but the National social religious work of parochial clergy will have no authority, and cease.

The position of our Church Schools is our most perplexing problem. The Free Education Act has not as yet disturbed them. In Nottinghamshire no additional requirements have been caused by it in 11 Deaneries ; in Southwell Deanery 3 buildings are ordered, in Mansfield 2, in Gedling 3. And a great work is required at S. Mary's Nottingham. There are 34 Board Schools, besides those at Nottingham. In the country the Fee Grant has caused gain rather than loss, and previous recent reductions of Fees in Nottingham itself enabled almost every school to be freed without loss. It is different in Derbyshire. Fees have been higher, and in the large proportion of schools in most Deaneries some additional school charge is continued. In Derby alone the schools could not be freed at less loss than £1500 a year. In only two Deaneries are there no new requirements of buildings caused. Possibly the change of Inspector has raised the standard for Infant Schools. Twenty-two schools have been built, or added now or enlarged, at an estimated cost of £13,000. The village districts seem supplied and maintained. In the populous places great efforts have had to be made—Staveley and Heanor are the chief examples, the latter having no less than nine schools, three of them built quite lately, and two more ordered. Besides Derby, there are 28 Board Schools. A considerable number of schools are in continual struggles. On the whole, however, the prospect of our Church Schools' stable maintenance is generally quite satisfactory, and I only know of one instance where building requirements threaten the creation of a Board, viz., the hamlets of Heath, where the schools have hitherto held, under Canon Cottingham, a conspicuous place in our religious examinations. In several instances the very able organising visitor, whom the Diocese had for two years, was able to improve schools from danger to safety. It was to my very great regret that Mr. Cox could not be retained by the Diocese, as his very complete mastery of school business and methods was capable of assisting the most experienced managers and masters.

For the special building requirements created by the Act, a Sustentation or Emergency Fund has been raised, which, with a valuable contribution from the S.P.C.K., amounted to about £2000, being about one-tenth of the estimated cost of the requirements. I have to thank the donors, among them the Duke of Devonshire for his leading gift of £300 ; and I believe the grants from the Fund will have given just the help and encouragement needed to bring a number of schools through the pressure.

The Schools question is, however, not one of this or that special pressure, except in the sense that a last straw breaks the camel's back. The two questions are (1) : Whether the coming masters will continue in the face of Board School management, and (2) whether the coming generation of Churchmen will continue to pay school rates and also subscribe. The question is only of great consequence in large School Board towns, which are also the places where the question is acute. There is a growing feeling, which I share, that in these large towns the issue will have soon to be decided by those ratepayers, who desire religious education, standing out for having their rates expended in accordance with their wishes, and changing ' the present settlement of the religious question,' as it is called. I think the ratepayers might claim with justice that the School rate should be distributed to all schools in proportion. Whether they will do so is another question. Parliamentary opportunists are not likely to lead the Crusade, and Churchmen are divided as to what signifies. There will be no united action, if ' the full Church teaching ' desired by Churchmen means a particular complexion of teaching about the Sacraments, the Ministry, and the position of the Church. No standard of religious school teaching will be enforced, which will not leave the clergy to teach the special Church teaching on these older subjects. That is their business, in my judgment. But if a School Board election may place a generation of children under regulations and teachers intended to exclude Christian knowledge from their school life, men who do not approve, may go to prison to maintain schools not so controlled. I have spoken on these subjects too often to be supposed to mean that Board Schools must be un-Christian. I do not believe that Universal School Boards would destroy Christianity, till it was destroyed without. But a centralized system gives the hasty stroke of a central pen too much power, and one man may under it destroy what generations could not replace. I know the weaknesses of an independent system. ' Every fool knows that.' But I know also the life and reality of liberty, and even the present School Board system may not inspire life learning or reality. It would ruin secondary education. However, this is off my subject. My value for Church Schools does not depend on their being teachers of Church Doctrine. I do not, however, see why arithmetic and history must be taught better, or deserve national or ratepayers' support better, *without* Church Doctrine than *with*. And I think that, if religious parents desire them to be taught *with*, the time has come for Churchmen to say that they see no reason why they should be the only people whose wishes receive no attention. Only, of course, they may have to go to prison.

The other public event affecting the Church in 1892 has been the termination of the protracted law suit of Read and Others *v.* Bishop of Lincoln. It is not my intention to criticize the judgment arrived at during four years deliberations. I accept it completely as the judgment not only of a Court determined by the chief authorities in Church and State to be competent, but also of a Court, which, if formed, as I think, on faulty principle, was nevertheless formed of the best men that could have been found in any way for the purpose. For the sake of the future I repeat now, what I desired to urge at the time, that I regret first that the Bishop of Lincoln did not feel the question ' What Court should try a Bishop in such matters ? ' to be one on which the Judges had a claim to hear both sides argued, and the Church and other Bishops had a claim, that both sides should be argued : and secondly I regret that when it was determined that the Court was the Archbishop, the Archbishop felt bound to imitate the method followed in the case produced as precedent, and did not feel that, having no form of Court prescribed by English law, he was left to follow the Church method and make the Court not of selected assessors, but of the Bishops of the Province. I regard the principle of ' selection ' for judicial purposes as vitally wrong, and liable to extreme abuse in partisan hands, however perfectly it may have been exercised on this occasion. The future is, however, I suppose, not irretrievably precedented down to this course, even by this precedent of following a bad precedent, and it may be hoped that, before another case arises, time may be given for fresh light to guide the then Archbishop or others to truer principles of Church jurydom. At the same time I do not question the least the competency of the Court composed. Still less do I assert any obligation that Church Courts, any more than Civil Courts, must be formed on one and the same model in all ages and churches. I think the ancient model for a bishop's trial more equitable than the latest modern.

I cannot say in which party's favour judgment has been given in the particular case. As in an ancient precedent, the Court seems to me to have awarded the parties a shell apiece. It must be hoped that, as in that precedent, the Court has obtained the solid object of contention ; its object having apparently been to effect a settlement. In regard to ourselves, the point on which judgment was declined, is the point on which the judgment most important to us is pronounced : in the declaration that even the Bishop of the Diocese, when visiting a church to join in its service, is not called upon to interfere then and there with the Incumbent's arrangements of the service, nor is he responsible for irregularities in them. That does not, of course, mean that it is not his office to correct irregularities : but he will do so at proper times, and not by distracting alterations on the spot. There may be irregularities extreme enough to justify immediate correction : the measure of such necessity would vary : but they are not probable at a bishop's visit without his previous knowledge. I feel that if a bishop were bound to take a model for uniformity everywhere with him, the distractions caused by his visits would make them more help than hindrance.

Very few of any party do not feel sorry that a man like the Bishop of Lincoln has been made party in such a trial, or fail to feel deep and sympathetic regret that his saintly work has been subject to such distractions and annoyances. His selection seems also to have been a blunder. Such trials will scarcely be repeated. Still I cannot withdraw my opinion expressed in my last charge that, at the time, though the disputed points had made their way into acceptance wide enough to disable prosecution, the prosecuting party were not to blame for pressing the legality of doubtful ceremonial, which perplexed and displeased many churchmen, to the fullest trial and judgment, believing, as they did, that parts at least had actually been pronounced illegal. I almost think that some judges of previous cases ought to share their costs. But the *arcanum imperii* has

D

been long revealed, that, in a civilized age, men have only to go to prison long enough, to baffle law, to abolish church rates (possibly, hereafter, school rates), and certainly to establish ceremonial. Prosecutions are an advance on the S. George's in the East riots : and if they produce the comfort that law is responsible for the established changes, they will have set both sides at ease. The Church will have been set by this judgment before trades unions in the race of progress, and been led to pass first through the barbarous stages of riots, imprisonments, and legislations, to the final arbitrement of Christian consideration and common sense.

Of the questions raised in that trial I will not speak at this point, for circumstances have caused me to put together at some length my thoughts upon some points in them which have come before me, and I shall make that statement a separate second part of this address. I will add a few words to conclude this.

I am not sorry to have been asked about the principles of Diocesan promotion. The one principle is Fitness. Length of service may mean length of merit or the reverse. Incumbents' choice of Curates depends very much on circumstances, and does not always prove fitness for livings. Seniority is the worst of all principles. Patrons are so often wanting men, that it is rare for a Curate who makes any mark by his work, not to be offered a post before he has served ten years. He will not expect to serve less. Many of our best Curates have refused posts offered them. Good work in the Diocese is the best claim for promotion in it, and yet work may be good without making a man fit for all posts, nor is parish work the only Diocesan work, or the only test of fitness. A Bishop's appointments should, more than any Patrons', shew an example of selecting the best man he can find for each particular place, and of regarding the place as the chief interest to consider. I find that I have had in these eight years to appoint to just 40 livings, and in 35 cases I have been glad to appoint clergy from the Diocese, three of the others being Hognaston, Kilvington, and Holy Trinity Ilkeston, which I was glad to find so good men to take, when clergy of the Diocese were not willing : the other two were the Metropolitan Churches of Nottingham and Chesterfield, for which I shall never feel my choice tied to the Diocese. A Bishop must strengthen his chief posts to his utmost. I rejoice to know that neither place has regretted my appointments to them. But my livings are not many, and if any County Legislator wishes to strengthen the Diocese, he should obtain a reversal of the ill-timed transference of the livings belonging to the Southwell

Minster, which, only just before this See was devised, were handed over to the new Bishoprics of Ripon and Manchester, simply because no one knew what to do with them. Those Bishops have a larger proportion of patronage to their clergy without them than this See would have with. If the scheme of that day was to equalize Bishops' Patronage, the new Sees give occasion for equitable revision. This transference of Patronage up to this time attached to our Cathedral seems pre-eminently to call for such revision. There are 15 of these livings in this Diocese, besides the numerous livings retained by the old Chapters of York, Lincoln, and Lichfield, though their connection with our counties has ceased. I have been unable to make a Chapter Act in which this revision could be embodied, because our Chapter has no property on which to base it. I hope the Laity will assist the Clergy to get this rectified. It affects the clergy and parishes more than the Bishop.

I have confirmed or preached in almost all our parishes. Retford and Wirksworth Deanery systems have left more churches near those towns than elsewhere as exceptions. Otherwise it has been only due to accidents or special difficulties, that any exception remains, except some half-dozen parishes too minute to find me an occasion—though I have welcomed small occasions for small parishes. I have much occasion to express great gratitude for the never-failing kindness with which I have been received on my visits, and the extreme care and hospitality both from Laity and Clergy, which has everywhere given me such pleasure and assistance. It would ill represent my feeling, to speak of the assistance mainly, but, when everything is done for me, I often think how impossible it would be without that friendliness, for a Bishop to do his office in a wide-lying Diocese, in days when hotels do not generally exist in reach. To mention them sounds out of place. And yet I cannot help sometimes feeling that I need the excuse of necessity for the inconveniences I must often cause my kind clergy, and for being unable to entertain them instead of being entertained by them. I pray them to accept my grateful thanks. It has been a great additional pleasure to meet so many parishioners with the clergy on these visits, and to find myself no longer a stranger, but to be able in most places to claim to recognize a number of old friends.

I am reminded in sending this address that my last Charge was completed on the day when I was taken ill, four years ago. This should have been issued earlier, but circumstances have delayed my last Visitation over into this new year.

It is food for a Bishop's reflection that in eight years I have become older in my See than any of the Bishops whose Dioceses touch this—Lincoln, Peterboro', Lichfield, Chester, Manchester, Wakefield, York. I have in nearly nine years ordained 217 clergy. Exactly 300 of the present list of not quite 700 clergy have entered the Diocese since I came at its formation. Seventy Incumbents out of 490 have died since my last Charge. Among them Archdeacon Balston, Canons Abney, Alderson, and Olivier, two Rural Deans of Glossop (Mr. Knowles and Mr. Bruce Ward), Mr. Chancellor, and Mr. Frith (Rural Deans of Derby and of Duffield) : our oldest Clergyman and Incumbent, Mr. Buckley, over 90 years, and 50 years Vicar of Hartshorne : at ages over 80 years, Mr. Humble (50 years at Sutton), Mr. Footit (nearly 50 years at Gonalston), Mr. Findley, Mr. Cantrell, Mr. Berry, Mr. Milnes, Mr. Waters, and just now Mr. S. Hey, nearly 50 years Vicar of Sawley, having served in the Diocese more than 63. Beside these 15 had been already disabled from active work. Of the others, many over 60 and over 70 had served long and were serving vigorously. But whereas in my last Charge, out of 52 I had but one quite young to record, and one more not in ripe old age ; this time the roll of those below middle age is no less than 16, including four devoted Curates (Mr. Hope, Mr. Sheffield, Mr. Lee, Mr. Hankey). Three I must name as suddenly taken from specially active work: Mr. Garbett, Mr. Bussell, Mr. Brown of Shireoaks.

Heavy as these losses among the Clergy have been, the losses among the chief Lay supporters of the Diocese has been even more exceptionally heavy. It must be very rare for a Diocese in four years to lose such exceptionally generous helpers as the Duke of Devonshire, Lord Carnarvon, Lady Ossington, Sir William Evans, Mr. Mackie, Mr. Mason, Mrs. Sherwin Gregory, Mrs. Robertson, the Misses Mosley, to which list I have to add the very special loss to myself, and also to the Diocese, by the death of the man who did more than any other single person to make the Diocese work together at first, the first Registrar, Mr. Watson.

These milestone periods of a Diocese cannot fail to have the sadnesses of all retrospects, but, as other retrospects, so must these be rather fresh starting-points for the ever-renewing body of the Diocese as for the individual successors to the vacant places.

The old Roman who built his house for everyone to see into, knew public life. The Church and her individual clergy gain by the full light upon them, if the light cast be not unfriendly colored. Weaknesses grow out of sight. Each enquiry is not only an opportunity for removing false impressions, but also an occasion for efforts to rise to the expectations presented by it. We have not all the same posts, no doubt. But the strength and honor of the Church is chiefly hazarded on those whose faithfulness to duty has least aid from public guard and stimulus. Parsonages should be, as very many are, the happiest as well as the best homes of England. Where they are so, their use needs no describing, any more than a candle set in its candlestick. A country lighted so would be madly set on darkness to throw them down. 'Let your light so shine before men,' is our call. The country does not want darkness, but it does want light. We have to walk as children of light—our people ask for light. There is our opportunity for service and its welcome. If a candle gives no light and needs removal, it is with sadness that is seen, not with ill-will—at least, ill-will stands condemned, and soon condemns itself. If threatening sounds are heard, that is the time for girding ourselves, as true men who, when the fight comes, feel the whole war depends each on his own self. In this war, if it does more than threaten enough to remind us that threatened men live long, the issue will rest with the villages. The Parochial system has been the life of the English Church by its penetrating through the villages, and it is to that penetration that the Church is still apt to point as her strength. That strength rests on those Village Parsonages being the best and happiest homes of the land, and on the light of teaching guidance and help, which shines from them. The country parson may feel left in an outpost. His post is the post of danger and of honor. May all be faithful to their hard post! What help and encouragement can be given them from Head Quarters it would be folly as well as crime for their Chiefs not to give. But it will not be on such encouragement that the duty of the most faithful will be based, but on their own hearts, unmoved, loyal trust, and allegiance to their own Master, to Whom alone they stand or fall, and Who has said to His servants whom He has put in trust for Him, and who have kept their trust, 'Well done! Good and faithful servant; thou hast been faithful over a few things, I will set thee over many things : Enter thou into the joy of thy Lord.'

II.

Though ritual questions are rare in the Midlands, circumstances have given me occasion to draw up, what I must not call a judgment but, an opinion, in reply to difficulties which have exercised the minds of some of my friends, not touching the legality, but rather the broader bearings of the disputed ritual, its tendency and motive, its meaning and value, and its popular impression. Of these broader bearings I would not speak in my last charge. The law case to which I have referred arose, and I deferred publication of my opinion till that should be decided. But now that it will not anticipate the Law and as I do not wish to criticize or discuss the Law, I prefer to say what I have been called upon to say, in the general and independent form in which I have for some time prepared my opinion. I may refer to later history at points, but I am not sorry to have worked rather on more ancient. It is after all only my reply to difficulties, which may well have become themselves ancient history. I believe that to be the case with the root-question, What is at issue in the disputes about ritual? Instead of asking merely, Is it Romish? people ask what is the meaning or use of it? To condemn things because they are done by Romans, is felt to be as foolish as to do things because they are done by Romans. There may be some affectation of being what it is the fashion to call 'Catholic-minded'; but outside that special ring, I believe that British insularity has given way at least enough to the disposition to consider without prejudice the merits of innovations in themselves. I say 'at least enough,' because I am sensible of a fallacy underlying the claim to judge each novelty by itself, as if there were no truth at all in small things being parts of great systems. The change of attitude is not unsuited to my opinion, which is indeed drawn from the same point of view. I am convinced that the mediæval developments from the Fourth Lateran, were rightly retraced by the Church of England when they were made Articles of Faith by the Council of Trent: that the rules of Clergy Celibacy and Refusal of the Cup to the Laity may have been at the time 'present necessities,' but are untrue and uncatholic as rules: that the systems of the Confessional and of Indulgences are fatally demoralizing: that worship of relics and Saints, and the Roman Sacramental Doctrines are grave errors. Practices, however small, which aimed at insinuating any of these points of the

Roman System would be in my judgment abandoning primitive truth for mediæval error. But I do not therefore assume that every revived usage 'involves such a retrogression, but consider the special subjects in dispute on their merits. Romanizing must be part of the question about each, but it enters in very different ways and degrees into the subjects of words, rules, and ceremonial, which form the heads of our discussion. Of these the words may be supposed to be least important, but they are even therefore the most important, as indicating a desire to innovate, not for the sake of some advantage such as may attach to rules or accessories in themselves, but simply to approximate to Romans.

I propose to discuss one word only, and to discuss it in regard to the principle underlying it in a more marked degree than the others which go with it. I mean the word Mass.

'Mass.' The revival of this name is said, 'if it has no other use, to mark the identity of the English and Roman Sacrament.' In itself it has no connotation. It appears to mean the Service which begins at the Missa or dismissal of the sets of people not admitted to Communicate. The Dismissal so began it and so named it. If the word connotes anything, it is the dismissal of all but the Faithful, who were all to communicate: and would not suit non-communicating attendance, or at least not that of children. I have heard it advocated as a short name of no special sacredness, and so more fit for common reference than the two Prayerbook names. Though this reason would not attach to devotional, official, or documentary references, it fits the English reserve, which shrinks from talking commonly of sacred names, as the Jews did not utter the Tetragrammaton. For commoner reference, however, our people have been satisfied with 'The Communion,' or more commonly, 'The Sacrament,' while a cultivated class has revived Eucharist, with a sense of something mystical about the untranslated name, which if it had passed through the same stages as. Communion has, would have been 'Grace.' Sacrament and Eucharist are the oldest names recorded by primitive writers after the New Testament. But the name Mass is revived (by an individual or perhaps Society use) avowedly as a mediæval name once common to both English and Roman churches. Our own last documentary use of it was the description of the Holy Communion as 'commonly called the Mass,' a phrase implying that such popular use was not legal or official.

Words differ from ceremonial; ceremonial may have merit apart from any ideas, while words can only be introduced for the sake of their idea. A church that has reformed may reform again, not only about customs and ceremonies, but about doctrine too, if it so determine. But if a name implies a doctrine, individual clergy are not free to introduce, still less to revive, such a name without their Church's authority. The revival implies two premisses. 1. That we ought to remove all needless marks of difference between the two Churches. 2. That the doctrine expressed by the word Mass is taught by the English as well as the Roman Churches, and, therefore, it is a needless mark of difference to use different names for the Sacrament. These premisses contain the controverted part of the ritual question, which is better discussed on words which have no other object, than on ceremonies which have independent value. Putting aside (as I propose to do throughout) all questions about legality, and with them the British motive to claim a right (even to ruin one's self) if thought to be improperly forbidden ; and asking what is supposed to be the gain in the use of the word Mass, I am met with ambiguity. It is never stated whether the object is Re-union with Rome, a return to Mediæval instead of Primitive Doctrine, or, while retaining our independence and doctrine distinct from Rome, to make a semblance of unity by using names in two different senses. The Re-union of Christendom is yearned for by Christendom : Re-union with Rome is, for ourselves, one of the nearest and main steps to that. But this is never professed to be the motive for mediæval revivals, but is indignantly denied to have any connection with them, and distinctions against Roman theories are drawn with no less skill than vehemence by the revivalists, leaving no doubt except about the sentiment and tendency which clothe and interpret their proceedings. I do not believe that any party in our Church desires to be absorbed into outer fringes of Rome, or regards an Italian Curia as England's true spiritual Directorate. Many would desire the communion which once existed : very few could accept the obedience which never existed. Speaking at this moment, not of doctrine, but only of the obedience, I do not wonder that sometimes when Church Government and Legislation are stifled, distance lends enchantment to the view of a spiritual power, independent of civil shackles : and if our Church ever lost its unique primitive basis of National Church, more men might come to think that rather than be one more local body, the second best would be to join, even in the lowest place, such an European Church combination for religion against Secularism ; but unless and until our Church is denationalized, few leading men will prefer to sacrifice our unrivalled opportunity to either phantasy or false history. Times recur in cycles, when good men, in despair of holiness, crave for spiritual despotism, which, however unfaithfully others have used it, they would exercise righteously; in despair of overcoming Atheism, crave for inquisitorial extinguishers, which, however faultily others have used them, they would put with unerring exactness on erratic liberty of thought; in despair of Church position, crave for an idealized world-wide Clergy Trades Union, in which, however others have been betrayed by power, they would be officers who would combine freedom and truth. But then, again, other times recur, when liberty and knowledge are trusted to be the instruments of truth and life; when it is seen that men desire truth even while floundering away from it in ignorance, and that truth is grown in liberty : when it is remembered that Church discipline has not maintained morality, nor Church repression unity. Oppressed churchmen turn ecclesiastic. But I don't believe them to desire to be directed from Rome, but to direct England so far as 'Catholic-minded' laymen require it of them. At any rate, as I began by saying, Union with Rome is repudiated by those thought to hoist its signals. Who could dream that words like Mass could make Union? The great questions with Rome are still, Is error to be stereotyped by a dogma of Church infallibility? And is liberty of thought to be suppressed by central Roman despotism?

I have supposed that my third alternative was the real account, viz., that men have wished to obliterate external differences of names and forms, and yet not meant to alter English teaching by doing so : or to put it another way, they have argued, These words and forms were used by England three centuries ago, and, therefore, may be used now. There may be Rip van Winkles so imbued with mediæval thought as to ignore modern meanings of such words and the impressions conveyed by them now, and to suppose that because mediævalists can naturally use them for what they meant in the Twelfth Century, therefore common people must be able to do so, though they have never known them mean any but the modern Roman sense. It is indeed not uncommon to hear it gravely argued that such revival of words in their old meanings would be an excellent Church history lesson—which it might be, if really so given. But to suppose ordinary people to be ready at once to take up an old meaning of Mass suited to English teaching, is as reasonable as to hold an argument with Sabbatarians on the basis of your treating Sabbath as meaning Saturday, because it once did so, and expecting them to understand you. If men mean to teach

Roman doctrine, that is another thing. But if they do not, as I have supposed, it seems a perversity, which may be almost called childish, to discredit themselves by misunderstandings wilfully created in their people's minds, and to disable their opportunities of influencing Englishmen with English teaching, merely for the sensational freak of startling unlearned helplessness by talking of Mass, seven Sacraments, and other disparagements of our Prayer-book and Articles. In times when our Church requires ' a strong pull altogether ' to carry her work through against real opposition, it is a great loss if any fine spirits, fit to be leaders, stop her progress and endanger her safety for the pleasure of ' kicking over the traces.'

Is it then, thirdly, to teach Roman Doctrine that men revive terms which have in common regard been specialized to Roman aspects ? Remember that I have said throughout that the revivers strongly repudiate this. The argument which I quoted at first may serve as a handle for the discussion. ' The word Mass will shew the identity of the English and Roman Sacrament.' In what sense is this true, and in what sense untrue ? It is one chief blessing of the very simple Sacramental acts and elements that they can be, and have been, repeated and spread the same through ages and languages in every way different, and the benefits of that memorial rest on the same Divine mercy, and tend to the same salvation of souls in all churches, however different their mode of appropriation or their measure of knowledge. This identity spreads beyond England and Rome, and is befitted by names of more complete primitive Catholicity than Mass. Is Mass used to exclude the identity of English and Eastern Sacrament, though English Church origins were Eastern? Mass is but a poor, non-Catholic, name of little meaning, compared with the grand old Sacramentum of Christian allegiance. Sacrament is not insular, but Catholic ; Mass is not Catholic, but Roman. It dwarfs the Catholic identity of the Sacrament. Mass does not identify the English with the Roman Sacrament, but only an English with the Roman special aspect of the Sacrament. Is it, then, true to do this ? Is it true that ' The Sacrifice of the Mass,' in the sense in which it is taught and understood by the Roman Church, is an aspect of the Sacrament identical with that of the English Church ? The essential part of this question is, of course, ' in the sense taught and understood in the Roman Church.' Definition of ambiguous words and distinction of confused meanings are, as I keep repeating, the remedies against fallacies. Sacrifice is most truly an English aspect of the Sacrament ; but not in the sense of sacrifice taught of the Roman Mass. Christ's Real Presence in the Sacrament is most truly an English aspect of the Sacrament ; but not in the sense taught by Rome in Transubstantiation. That communicants receive the Body and Blood of Christ is most truly the English teaching of our Catechism : but not materially in the Bread, as Rome teaches, but spiritually in the Sacrament. To revive the name Mass is to identify these opposite aspects of three chief points in the Sacrament. It is true that popular interpretations are often perversions of scientific teaching, and scientific Roman theology may not have meant what it has been understood to mean, that each ' Sacrifice of the Mass ' was a fresh actual repetition of Christ's immolation ; but that is the popular acceptance of its meaning, and that our Church rejects in every part of her service. Those among us who dwell most on the Atonement must be the first to feel that, as all Christian worship, so specially its most special act, will always plead in its remembrance of Christ His one full, perfect, and sufficient sacrifice, oblation, and satisfaction for the sins of the whole world : they will reverence the sacred Feast as the ever repeated Feast attendant on that one Sacrifice in memorial of Him. They will be emphatic in acknowledging the worshipper's part in the Sacrament, in oblations, in the praise and thanksgiving, and the offering of himself, his soul, and body, which the service calls sacrifices. If there is no concealment (and why should any be supposed ?), no school in our Church teaches any Sacrifice in the Sacrament beyond these several intentions. But then they are not the Roman teaching of the Sacrifice of the Mass, nor can that name be used of them with propriety and without confusion. Again, it is true that the old scholastic terms, ' Transubstantiation ' and ' Real Presence,' have (like the later word ' Objective ') come by changes in thought and words to mean the very opposite to what they meant when invented for the Sacrament. No more ingenious application of the philosophy of the day to explain the inexplicable was ever made than in the term Transubstantiation. But it did not teach the, at least, popularly supposed present Roman meaning of the term, that Christ's human flesh and blood are materially eaten in the Sacrament. To us, in our modern use of language about ordinary men, a person's being really present means that he is there in his material body of solid parts, skin and bones and so on, which we call substantial. But in the exploded philosophy of the schoolmen, man's reality or substance meant just the reverse : it meant the special characteristic which constituted a being a man, which was supposed to form an impalpable substratum of his existence, of which the senses could have no cognizance. Flesh and blood and all that we call substances were not man's reality or substance, but mere appendages, which would not have been called substantial. If Transubstantiation has been caused by modern change of language to mean the opposite of its original intention, so that its modern meaning that Christ's material Body, His natural Flesh and Blood, are materially eaten in the elements, is really a popular caricature of a great Church's scientific teaching, there may be nothing in Transubstantiation but an exploded philosophic explanation of transcendental metaphysics, about which it would not be worth while to dispute. But it would be a strange thing then for us to talk popularly of Mass, which is so popularly misunderstood, and which, rightly understood, means only something exploded. In that case, if Rome could repent even enough not to be a slave to words' changed meanings, she would probably abandon terms belonging to an exploded philosophy. But she cannot. As it is, the word Mass conveys to popular understanding the two ideas, that Christ is slain afresh each time the Sacrament is ministered, and that the nature of the Bread and Wine is metamorphosed into Christ's natural Flesh and Blood. This cannot by any means be called identical with our Church's teaching, which contradicts both ideas most explicitly in her service and articles. No less clearly is the adoration of the elements, ordered both for priest and people in the Roman Rubrics, condemned in ours. How can ' Mass' be said to show the identity of the English and Roman Sacrament ?

I have said that it is most truly English teaching that Christ is truly present in the Sacrament, and the term Real Presence is usable by us in our modern understanding of the word real to mean true and actual, as well as in the scholastic meaning of real as essential. But whereas the Council of Trent anathematizes all who say that Christ is only partaken in a spiritual manner, our Church teaches that His true and Essential Presence is Spiritual, and that Communicants receive Him in a Spiritual manner and Sacramentally in the Sacrament. Our Church's language in Articles and Catechism may be thought to admit two possible Theories of Sacramental instrumentality : but if so, neither of them is that of the Roman Mass.

I do not doubt our Church's teaching to be that Sacramental instrumentality is Spiritual, as I read that of the primitive Church to have been : teaching that the Bread and Wine are 'antitypes signs and symbols' of Spiritual Food not identical with them but represented by them, so that our spirits receive the operation of the Spiritual Food as our bodies of the material. The act of Sacramental worship faithfully offered in the symbolic representation ordained by Christ for His memorial, strengthens and refreshes the soul with 'the Spirit that quickeneth,' and which is the real substance and real Presence of Christ. The Spirit and thoughts of Christ, the Word or Mind of God, is our Spirit and Life, as they are Himself. Making memorial of Christ in thankful remembrance and in full assurance of Faith, we feed in our hearts by faith with thanksgiving. Present He has promised to be truly in our united worship, to make His disciples' hearts burn within them, as the ordained means of fitting symbols, prayers, thanksgivings, memorials, beliefs, thoughts, agencies, which combine for Sacramental worship, bring their spirits into communion with His Spirit and feed them with the living Bread of the Spirit of Christ, making His Spirit ours, His thoughts our thoughts, His life our life, Himself one with us. I believe this to be the Sacramental teaching of our own Church and of the primitive Church. It is difficult to draw an intelligible line between Transubstantiation and other theories identifying the sign and the thing signified, which might bring the latter outside of the criticism of our Article that Transubstantiation overthrows the nature of a Sacrament. I am properly at this moment only concerned with the fact that all such other theories are not the Roman theory and cannot properly be called by the name Mass. Still I will not leave out of this discussion the second Sacramental theory thought to be admissible by the words of our Church's somewhat uncertain documents. I am prepared to say that I only see two extreme views entirely excluded by all our Church's language—that of a social meal, and that of adoration of the material elements. In such transcendental mysteries, which can be brought to no test, I would not wish to exclude any interpretation which has meaning, if it can be brought within our Church's language. It is very difficult to analyse theories on so sacred a subject, and still more to express that analysis, without being thought irreverent. How and when Grace is given in the Sacrament might well have been left unasked. But it is too late to wish that, and a comparison of theories cannot avoid close and distinct analysis and statement. The second theory, thought admissible by our Church's language, is, that consecration attaches Christ's Spiritual Body to the material elements of Bread and Wine, so that, while they still remain God's creatures

F

of Bread and Wine, Christ's nature is united to them. This is what is really meant by the Lutheran theory of Consubstantiation, and as such it may claim the large Lutheran body as accepting it. About this theory I will not ask questions of transcendental metaphysics, which might seem to be answered in mystical language. But an attempt to grasp the precise theory makes it seem to contain two parts, which challenge reasonable consideration, but about which I only propose to ask for their authority. They are : 1. That the act of consecration, by virtue of power conferred on a Priest in Ordination, has miraculous power, independent of the spirit of minister or recipient, whereby Christ's very Body is, without fail, brought down from heaven and attached to the material Bread and Wine ; and 2. That Sacramental Grace operates on the soul through effects on the body, produced by the elements so changed by consecration. Mysteries cannot be brought to test, and I refrain, as I said, from questioning the meaning of the miracle taught. But what authority is there for this miraculous power, claimed for every priest alike, and for the words and acts of consecration ? It is not irrelevant to observe that different churches attach consecration to different parts of the Liturgy, the Eastern to the invocation of the Spirit, the Western to the recitation of the narrative of the Institution, which was at first only recitative. There is no formula of universal use as in Baptism. But apart from this, the extreme power claimed for the priestly act requires very clear authority for its acceptance. That priests are solemnly adjured to bear in mind the tremendous solemnity of ministering the Sacrament, and that the rhetoric of such Greek patristic adjurations is carried to an ecstatic extreme, is very true, but Greek rhetoric is as figurative as literal, and what is no exaggeration about the ideal ministration of so great a Sacrament, and the dignity of the true priest's instrumentality in such a work of Divine Grace, is not a theological definition of Sacramental operation, nor a statement that the mere words and acts of any priest, simply as priest, have the stupendous power claimed for them. Can we think that the New Testament would leave such a power unnoticed ? After paying the fullest regard to the nature of the New Testament books, and to the fact that things may be too well known to be noticed in such books, it is nevertheless difficult to suppose that such a principle of really vital character could fail to have had some notice in them if it had been known to the Apostles. Finding, too, as we do, in them discussions on reverence for the Sacraments and on reverence for the ministry, a principle vital to the character of Sacraments and ministry would have formed too important an element in such discussions to be wholly absent from them. The miraculous Sacramental power claimed by the theory under our discussion is presented in that theory as so vitally essential that the Apostolic age must have known it. But yet no sign of this gift appears in the New Testament, neither in discussions even of questions of which it would have been the key, nor among the specimen gifts of Grace, nor among the specimen offices, nor among the specimen charges and powers devolved by S. Paul on Timothy and Titus. It is difficult to think this a doctrine that would have been left to mediæval development. It is needless to say that I am not now treating of the priestly dignity and office of Offering the Sacrifice of the Liturgy. That belongs to a separate discussion.

It is more difficult to speak without reserve of the second point named above, viz., the theory which I have identified with what was intended by the Lutherans in the obsolete term Consubstantiation. The authority for this consists of a number of of Patristic passages of three kinds. 1. Statements identifying the sign and thing signified. These form the ambiguity, about which interpreters will continue to differ, whether they imply material, or are satisfied by spiritual reality. But as they all rest on the words of the institution, those words had better be treated as their representative. 2. Inferences, in answer to the question, Where is the grace of the Sacrament contained? 3. Statements that after consecration the Bread does not remain mere or common Bread. I will speak shortly of these three arguments.

1. The words of the institution are said to compel a literal understanding of them, and it is called an evasion to take them in any but a materialistic sense. Much has been said of their grammar, and yet the most natural question about their grammar is ignored, i.e., whether in the sentence called the Words of Institution the ordinary rule of Greek grammar does not make 'This' the predicate, and make the sentence mean, My Body is this, i.e., My Body is Bread, i.e., no Paschal lamb shall be slain in remembrance of Me, but, as in Abel's sacrifice, and as in the unbloody offerings, the first fruits of the ground shall be offered. I shall not insist on this grammar, but it will be remembered that Irenæus speaks in the sense so given, ' Counselling His disciples to offer to God first fruits from His creatures, that they might not be unfruitful or ungrateful, took that which of His creation is bread, and gave thanks, saying, This is My Body.' ' How shall they know that that Bread, over which thanks are given, is the Body of

their Lord, if they do not acknowledge Him as the Son of the Creator of the World ? *i.e.*, His Word, through which wood yields fruit and the earth yieldeth first the blade, then the ear, then the corn in the ear.' (Ir. iv., 17.5.) The catena of passages down to S. Augustine quoted by Pusey on the Real Presence on the point 'He called Bread His Body,' may be spoken in the same sense. Without dwelling however on this, it must needs be recognised that the sentence of Institution does not stand in the air, as if it were a definition from controversial theology, but is circumstanced by the Paschal scene and the Passion, yet unknown but now to follow, and the contrast of the two memorials. Those who call it an evasion to interpret the sentence in any but a material sense, must at least remember that all the epigrams pointed at the so-called evasion said to be made by spiritual interpretation, apply with equal force to any even the most extreme Roman interpretation, which stops short of asserting that communicants eat materially Christ's human flesh. This admits direct appeal to sense. But pretended Roman miracles of making blood flow from a consecrated wafer shew to what the literal interpretation comes. The passage most rested upon is the Chapter of S. John, which says, ' Except ye eat *My Flesh.*' I can only read that chapter to declare explicitly that these words are to be taken spiritually, and seeing how much is made to rest on the interpretation of that chapter as referring to the Sacrament, I suppose that the words of the Institution will be admitted to bear the same interpretation. The ambiguous patristic identifications depend on this first and chief example.

2. ' The Grace *must be* in the Elements, *for where else can it be?*' This represents the second argument, which does not profess to follow authority, but to rest on its own inference, stated as if exhaustive, and as nothing else but a logician's exhaustive inference, open to criticism of its exhaustiveness. It would be enough to answer, Why not in the Sacramental action, which was really the Memorial instituted by Christ ? But the Sacramental theory of a Real Spiritual Divine Presence promised to such Christian assemblies in His Memorial is our Church's loftier interpretation.

3. There remain the passages which speak of the consecrated Bread as not mere or bare or common bread. But will this carry such a stupendous theory as that of which we are speaking ? No school in our Church would speak as if consecration left it *mere or common* bread, with no special character attached to it. A consecrated building remains a building, but not the *mere* building, but a Church with instrumental power to raise souls in worship. A silken banner remains silk, but not *mere* silk, but a

nation's representative of honor to be guarded with her soldiers' lives. The wedding ring is still the gold, but not *mere* gold, but the wife's most precious emblem, never to be parted with. Ordained men are still men, but are, like Churches, made by their office to uplift souls and represent the Church in worship. If in these instances the power of consecration be subjective, it is not therefore unreal or imaginary.

I know that the Spiritual theory of the Sacrament has been called Subjective, and in that word has been meant to be called unreal. It has been called a *low* view, and the materialist theory a *high* Sacramental theory. Men have argued in would-be epigrams, that virtual Presence is real absence. But these criticisms rest on ideas strangely out of accord with the teaching that 'God is a Spirit, and they who worship Him must worship Him in Spirit to worship Him in reality.' Materialism may call spiritual impressions subjective illusions, but spiritual religion would be in strange confusion, if it called spiritual Communion 'subjective,' in the sense of 'imaginary,' because it is 'subjective,' in the sense of 'felt by the persons.' When the question is asked, Are subjective impressions adequate to the expectation of a Real Presence? in all reverent considerateness for mystical imagination striving to conjure up some palpable presentation, must we not ask, Is it indeed an elevating imagination to esteem a material impression upon substances as higher than a spiritual visitation to souls? What is the meaning of the desire for more than (to use the disparaging term) subjective impressions which are the only possible manifestations to our souls of that Spiritual Impressor's visitation and presence? If feeling craves some easier mode of apprehension, is it higher (I do not say, 'Is it more matter for Faith, by which Christ is to dwell in our hearts?') but is it *higher* to seek satisfaction in an imagination that God can be localized at will by man in a material substance? Is it not higher to strain our imperfect spiritual apprehension to believe what is spiritual to be real? A belief in a spiritual indwelling of Christ could not turn for satisfaction to the idea of a material presence. Ultimately our interpretation of 'Real Presence' will depend on our belief in Spiritual Reality, Personality, Presence and Communion. This must be matter for Belief. Test, Proof, Analysis, Knowledge of Christ's method of Communion are impossible. Disputations about such mysteries might well have been counted the last things to justify divisions. But that is no longer possible. To return at last to the point which has led to this more serious discussion. To adopt the name Mass is not now to decline disputation, but to change sides upon it. It would not mean 'Don't dispute, but communicate.' It means, 'Accept the Roman view.'

I pass, without touching at this moment other Words, to speak of some Customs or Rules which have caused questions.

Here the principles assumed require chief notice. It is an often assumed opinion that Catholicity requires universal uniformity in observance of customs (and those not Apostolic only, but Ecclesiastical), which usage at some early period is said to present as Catholic, even although (or still more, if) no Canon or Decree ever made the practice a rule. This is stated as a truism, but it contradicts our Article which declares that Churches have right to ordain their own rites and ceremonies. And men who magnify S. Augustine's place in making the Church in England and S. Gregory's in sending him, ought to respect the instruction of S. Gregory to S. Augustine, that he should introduce what customs would suit the English. It has, however, become a root question, Are Church practices to be enforced because they are rules, or because they are good ? For children, for the weak and ignorant, for beginners, rules as rules are good in religion as in everything, for aids and scaffolding. But that is not the question, but whether for Churchmen who are what S. Paul calls Perfect, good churchmanship means, in its perfection, keeping rules, or doing what is best. It is not a question either of doing in regulated order, what has to be done by many in common. It is the question, what gives character to Church practices ? Is it their spiritual helpfulness, or their having formed somewhere at some time a custom ? It is S. Paul's old question about Law, or rather the older question which the Pharisees answered one way and Christ the other. Our Church says that customs may rightly differ in different countries. We think that religion is not only richer and more living for such variations, but is also more effective in each country from such adaptation. Japanese are not European by wearing French hats, nor are Englishmen Catholics by using Eastern hours. In things not affected by country, men may be uniform ; in things affected by country, they ought to be different. To make Easter uniform with Rome was a wise English concession for unity of action : to insist on Southern Fasting in England is as unwise as it would be to insist upon Immersion in Baptism. To have Seasons for Common Fasting is again wise : but to make individuals' Fasting identical is as unwise as to make their frequency of Communicating. Age for Confirmation and Communion, and hours for services, are examples of things independent of other churches, which each should regulate for itself. Clergy Celibacy and Refusal of the Cup to the Laity are examples of Roman non-Catholic rules, justified doubtless by circumstances at the time when the rules were made, but camels to gnats in comparison with an unmixed Cup or non-Fasting Communion. English clergy liberty about marriage and beards is better law than Greek or Roman contradictory regulations. And yet there are symptoms of the Roman rule being adopted as more truly clerical. To call an useful practice a rule, may help observance of a good thing. But the time may come when it will be supposed to be done not for its usefulness, but as a prescription even if worse than useless. Then ' whoso looketh into the perfect law of liberty ' will denounce such rule as false in spirit, and degrading spiritual religion into formal.

' Fasting Communion.' Consider now first the prescription to Communicate fasting. The materialistic and Manichæan ideas on which this has been sometime since urged, are withdrawn at present, and I hear it urged now only as a rule. It is publicly alleged that there are teachers who still call non-fasting Communion 'mortal sin.' But generally representative advocates of the rule admit that it is not suited for all English Communicants. ' But make it,' they say, ' a rule, subject to Bishops' dispensations.' This puts the obligation on an entirely different level, from which we may discuss it. Now I don't think dispensations all untrue or valueless. Vows may be taken subject to adequate independent judgment that changes oblige their termination, and, if taken on that express condition, are freed by it from vows' two opposite weaknesses. But unless dispensations belong to individual cases and particular reasons, they are not dispensations, but abrogations of the rule. In England it is whole classes who are excommunicated by a rule of Fasting Communion. Dispensations for whole classes are admitted to be necessary from age, health, or circumstances. If the only object would be, after all, to make a rule, what is the sense of making it to abrogate it ? If the rule supposed were a rule recognizing limitations of age, health, and circumstances, that would be different. Though the truer principle for hour and preparation would be ' worship when and as you can worship best.' Strong young people may worship best early and fasting : aged and weak cannot. Besides, the Communion is not an individual's service, but one essentially united, and it may often be a higher law for children to join parents in it than to suit their own separate interest. Again, frequent Communion is better than Fasting Communion, which tends to reduce frequency. Busy hard-worked people can't fast with advantage : nor can distances admit of it. Even the clergy are frequently exhausted by it to a degree that hinders their office. Fasting is a different thing in this country from what it is in Southern lands, where men live on nothing and do but little. Putting aside, however, all reasons against the particular rule of Fasting being pressed in England now, however general a custom it was in Africa in S.Augustine's time, the root idea of enforcing Ecclesiastical rules as rules, without regard to their suitableness, is itself more contrary to Christian wisdom than any branch example. Ecclesiasticism is not an advance upon the spiritual liberty of doing the best, but retrogression from it. Such rules touch the wrong persons. Many people are better for fasting, many more would be ; but rule binds just those who are worse for it. The spirit of reverence will begin the day with the Sacrament, if that is felt its best reverence : but yet it is also another not untrue or unacknowledged principle of reverence, that what should be most honored should belong to the most frequented hour of public worship. For the Clergy whose lives are framed by and for their ministration, for the strong, young, free members of society, hours are easy which are fixed by and for them : but those hours may be very arbitrary. They may not be working men or women's hours, nor hours for England. Indeed, to make hours Catholic, the course of the Sun must change. Much has been done in our lifetime to increase reverence for the Sacraments and all worship. But this was done by example, not by rule. We thank the earnest generation which revived the reverence and living worship which we have enjoyed. But even therefore we object to rule being made supreme, and to the spirit of that generation being lowered to externalism. Of course materialistic ideas of the Sacrament introduce special reasoning about fasting before it : but in themselves those ideas might as well prohibit eating after as before, and if the rules in question are made for the sake of those ideas, that makes them after all mere rules, settled arbitrarily, as rules are, and only as a particular way of satisfying the idea. Those materialistic reasonings I do not discuss here. They are not now professed to be the motives insisted upon. People believe them still to be the motives, because the Roman system seems to make them so. But the old idolization of Rule is deeper still, and a change from Romanising to Judaizing principles is very easy, and I believe the present phase is to magnify Compulsory Catholicity of rule above Christian liberty of principle. If the Church has no power to adapt practices and ceremonies to times and countries, it is not a living body but a dead machine. Rule pressed by casuistry becomes Rabbinism.

An example of this is shewn in a Mesopotamian Bishop's casuistical Canon of the Sixth Century produced in advocacy of the rule's obligation. ' If a man is troubled with sore throat, let him put his trust in God, who will cure him without his gargling, if he abstain from gargling out of reverence for the consecrated Gifts.' ' Comment ' (says the writer from whom I quote) ' is needless.' S. Chrysostom, in his well-known passage, appealed to by both sides, is surely healthier ; who, while asseverating, that he had never himself celebrated except fasting, repudiated the teaching that fasting was essential. S. Paul's casuistry meets the case best : ' He that eateth, eateth to the Lord, for he giveth God thanks ; and he that eateth not, to the Lord he eateth not, and giveth God thanks. Let every man be persuaded in his own mind.' Apply this principle to our question, and it says : ' If fasting helps your spiritual worship, fast. If it hinders it, don't. Worship with your body as well as your spirit : but all bodies are not the same body. Fasting gives life to pampered bodies, but from exhausted bodies it takes away even the life that they have.' I do not speak against ' fasting Communion,' but against *a rule of* fasting Communion. Were that rule based on materialistic ideas of profanity attaching to Non-fasting Communion, that would be, as I have said, a deeper question, but as it is not so based now, I only say that such materialistic ideas are not the teaching of our Church.

It is most strange to find the rigorous rule of Fasting before the Communion rested upon the letter of S. Augustine to Januarius (Ep. 54), which has been hitherto regarded, and it seems rightly, as the earliest authority for the existence of the custom. The whole spirit of the letter, written to a young secretary who was troubled about rules, is to state the liberty of churches to vary points not ruled by the Apostles or ' plenary councils,' such as keeping anniversaries of Christ's Passion, Resurrection, and Ascension, and the Descent of the Holy Spirit : and the Christian wisdom of conforming to the customs of Churches where you visit. ' First I would have you hold, what is the key of this discussion, that our Lord says that His yoke is easy and His burden light.' Days of Fasting, Frequency of Communions, are His own examples of customs open to variety, of which he says that ' it is the best rule for a sober Christian to act as the Church acts where you are.' ' I am often grieved at weak brethren being troubled by some brother's contentious obstinacy or superstitious fear, stirring such litigious questions as to think only their own way right.' How can this letter be made a text for rigorous Catholic rule ? The question about the Eucharist arose from Januarius asking if we are not bound to receive after food, because the Institution was after Supper. S. Augustine replies, ' It is true that the Disciples did not receive fasting at the Institution. But does that justify your censuring the whole Church, if people receive fasting now ? If Christ had ordered it to be always received after food, I don't suppose any one would have varied the custom.' So far he presents his argument as his own. His incidental reference to the custom as existing is what the letter contributes to the history of the practice. He then adds two points which are often accepted as no less established by his words, and on which the main stress is laid. 1. That S. Paul may be understood to have altered the hour. 2. ' That it seemed good to the Holy Ghost ' (using the words of the Council at Jerusalem) ' that in honor of so great a Sacrament the Lord's Body should enter the Christian's mouth before his other food.' But both these statements are his own inferences based simply on the custom being general, and solemn as the words sound, we must not magnify them to be more than S. Augustine's own. Solemn as the words sound, we must remember that the letter is not a solemn letter to the Church, but to a young man who wished to set the Church right : and the spirit of the letter is not to insist on the obligation of the custom, but to tell the young man that it was silly to find fault with settled custom. Further, the reason given by S. Augustine for the custom does not allege the Ascetic idea of fasting being a necessary purificatory preparation for the Eucharist. He gives no hint of pollution in eating, or holiness in fasting, which would make it profanity to receive non-fasting. This Ascetic idea, which has been revived among us, is not present in S. Augustine's, any more than in S. Cyprian's, argument for Early Communions. It was not our Lord's teaching, nor His Apostles'. When we remember the superstitious views about fasting bequeathed by the Jews, and that Africa of all Churches was most Ascetic in its teaching, it seems impossible that if the Ascetic reason was in S. Augustine's mind, he should not have uttered it here. Fasting was required before Baptism of a convert, but no early rules ordered it before the Eucharist, nor does S. Augustine order such preparation here. His feeling appears, in the earlier part of the letter, in his discussion of daily Communion. On one side it was argued, Men should choose days on which they live with special self control. On the other, If men's sins do not deserve excommunication, they ought not to withdraw from ' the daily medicine ' of the Lord's Body. S. Augustine says, Above all, abide in the peace of Christ ; let each do what he is persuaded in his own mind to be best. *Contemptum solum non vult cibus iste.* So S. Augustine's reason to justify the change from ' after Supper ' (which Januarius would have revived) to ' before other food,' was ' in honor of so great a Sacrament.' An honor of precedence, which still remains a valid argument, and which was satisfied by the Christian Liturgy beginning the ferial part of each day. But this is quite apart from the Ascetic idea of fasting. And the whole letter contradicts the idea of rule as rule.

In speaking against rigorous rule, I seem to differ in word rather than in meaning from the advocates of Rule mitigated by Dispensation. I do not now question early usage, but universal obligation. Supposed obligation is made practically a ground for excommunicating great numbers of our people. When the supposition of a rule deters priests (in consideration of their own case) from Celebrating after breakfast, Dispensation must be regulated on some new principle to meet the case. It is this obligation of an alleged rule which is our concern. Rule as it has been called, for the Church generally it was only an indefinite custom at the most, so far as any evidence has been given. But suppose it all that its advocates call it, yet if they say that the obligation admits of Dispensation, can they call the rule one of such sacred character that its violation would be profanity ? If I believed the materialist reasons alleged for the rule, I could not give Dispensation from what would then be not a matter of individual fitness, or ecclesiastical regulation, but of principle and of the nature of the Sacrament, which no Dispensation could affect. But if the rule can admit such an amount of Dispensation as is needed in England to avoid an intolerable system of Excommunication, it befits our Church better, in my judgment, not to ordain a rule which involves such alternative consequences.

' Non-Communicating attendance. ' This practice might naturally seem one to be advocated by people in proportion as they attach least Sacramental effectiveness to the elements, and regard the service most as a purely spiritual one of prayer and praise and thanksgiving. It is not in accord with the institution, nor with the principles of S. Paul's arguments. It seems to weaken the individual's participation, responsibility, and corporate unity. The prayers are not adapted for use by Non-Communicants. The dismissal of all but the Faithful in old Liturgies gives no encouragement to it. The reasonableness of such half Communion in assemblies of ill-regulated masses is intelligible ; as that of refusing the Cup was, and would still often be, in elementary churches. But in that respect both practices seem more fitly temporary than perpetual regulations. Full, separate, individual administration to great numbers is very wearing, not to priest so much as to people. The diminution of frequency in communicating, from daily breaking of bread to once at Easter or three times in the year, has these practical causes, which seem ready to influence advice and system again in our own time. It is not only imitating foreign ways or adopting foreign ideas. Rules of fasting and confession necessarily restrict Communions. If the whole Church communicated regularly under those rules, successive armies of celebrants and confessors would be required by the mere conditions of time : armies of Bishops to grant or refuse Dispensations. But I do not doubt that the practice is part of a wish to follow the Roman practice of making Mass the one chief service. That is a practical question, worthy of fuller consideration than it often receives. No service is so complete as the full Communion Service in its surroundings of its chief central Memorial. Now that hymns have ousted the Psalms from their place as interludes, it is true that the Old Testament has in it only its standing Lesson, the Commandments. But the selected double course of New Testament passages for the year, pointed by their Collects, the fuller Creed, the Sermon, and the very full and special Exhortations, form our fullest instruction : the preparation prayers and special Confession, Absolution, Comfortable Words, and Humble Access, with the comprehensive Intercession of the Prayer for the Church Militant, are our Church's best Prayers. No form of Praise and Thanksgiving surpasses the Sanctus, the Gloria, and Post Communion Collects. The whole service presents, in our Church's highest embodiments, all that Mattins contains, besides its special chief office of Offertory and Memorial and Communion. Set with some great master's music, that service, full and complete, is by far our noblest service, and might well be the one Morning Service for the Faithful. Only this is generally simply an impossibility for our people as a service of fasting Communion. Without Communion, it is only instruction, and no service of prayer or confession, praise or thanksgiving. That must be added by Mattins. That the congregation should never hear the Commandments as their standing Sunday Lesson, I believe to be a greater loss than our clergy recognize. That they should not hear the Collect, Epistle, and Gospel, is cutting off their Christian year's lessons, in which they ought to hear the whole Gospel. I regret these results of Early Communions, where they follow. But clearly the Ante-Communion Service without Mattins is a very poor modicum of prayer and praise. And Matins were made for that very purpose as a people's service. The union of the Services represents what is presumed to have been the earliest practice by those who assert that Christians never met in their assemblies without the Communion. For the Synagogue worship, which Mattins present, was clearly part of their assemblies' worship. Our practice of holding one immediately after the other was ordered for the convenience of the people : as in hill countries Morning and Evening Services have been taken without break, to have them finished and get home. But it was nothing unprincipled or unprimitive. And for ordinary people it seems now most acceptable, and is not any more unprincipled. Still, though this is all true, I think it also true that for Communicants no Sunday Service can better occupy the chief place than the Communion Service alone, if full and complete, and that none admits more properly of the fullest accessories as a joyous Service of praise and thanksgiving. I say ' for Communicants.' It is not, like fasting, a simply personal question. Non-Communicants mar the Service's perfectness for the Communicants, as well as destroy the corporate meaning of the Church Institution. However a body of Communicants can and will allow one another. But it is a different thing to make the Communion a Priest's performance before a miscellaneous congregation, which is sometimes desired. Our Service, containing no dismissal of Catechumens, penitents or others, but only exhortations against careless Communions, does not rubrically exclude Non-Communicants ; Cranmer, in fact, was afraid to go so far in the way of sudden reform, as to require all to receive, or depart. But later, the removal of what notices of departure existed, is ascribed to the practice of non-communicating attendance having ceased, so that they were needless. Instead of which, omission to direct people to go is taken to mean prohibition of their going. If history is brought to interpret some Rubrical questions, why is it nothing here?

As regards primitive practice, the rule seems clearer in this matter than about Fasting Communion, and certainly to go back beyond any date assigned to that, even to the New Testament. Those who make Fasting Communion essential *as a rule*, have to explain why the rule is not essential that all present should receive. Dangers have attached to both Non-fasting Communion and Non-communicating attendance. If the latter is not forbidden by our Church, neither is the former. If the former is against early practice, so is the latter : and whereas the former can only be traced to an uncertain date, the latter is against a principle as well as practice of the New Testament. If the latter is revived with the view of imitating the Roman practice of 'assisting at the Communion' or 'hearing Mass,' and so identifying the Roman and English Sacramental theories, I have spoken enough on that subject. If the practice is introduced because pious souls find spiritual benefit in such half-communion at times, let no rule hinder them as a rule. Let the Communicants bear with their imperfect sympathies and union, and if some justifying principle or precedent for their presence is wanted, regard them as penitents half restored. The Rubrical order to arrange the Communicants in convenient position before the Communion, should prevent the hindrances commonly caused by having them mixed in crowds of Non-Communicants. But I believe people to be quite wrong who suppose Rome to think 'hearing Mass' to be the better custom, or that it is more than a survival from past necessities, or that Rome would now begin Non-communicating attendance, or be otherwise than amused if we should take this, amongst other necessities or exaggerations or abuses, for her deliberate example. Whether adults are brought by the practice nearer to becoming Communicants I have no means of judging. That is its best argument. It needs evidence. But of unconfirmed children I feel strongly, that their presence contradicts Church principle, and by confusing them about their Church position, endangers instead of promoting their readiness to be confirmed and so become Communicants, when they seem to themselves to have been so already as much as older people round them. If the purpose be to transform the idea of the service into that of a propitiatory Sacrifice in which the priest alone is to take part, and the people to be only passive spectators, no idea is more opposed than this to the practice and principles of the primitive churches.

'Evening Communions.' I cannot speak from any personal experience about these. I have never been present at one. Personally I feel repugnance to them. This may be from habit, but I do not think my instinct is mere prejudice. When, however, they are spoken of as 'Shocking,' I have never been able to feel such language compatible with the circumstances of the original Institution. I might for myself adopt in regard to them the attitude of S. Chrysostom, who guarded his judgment about Non-Fasting Communion, by asseverations that he had never himself joined in it, "but if anyone called it 'sin,' let him then degrade Christ Himself." The change of hour for the Eucharist from the Evening hour of the original Institution to the hours of main

Church custom is well known to be obscure and uncertain both as to its facts and its reasons. It is not clear or necessary that the hour was at first the same everywhere. Christians followed their country's method of counting days: the Jews' and Greeks' Day began at sunset, the Roman at midnight. If the Eucharist began the Day, its hour may have been different at first in different countries, and only made uniform, as Easter was, later and for uniformity's sake. The letter of Pliny about Bithynia may be irrelevant to Corinth and other places. There is no evidence whatever for the assumption that S. Paul altered the hour at Corinth at the time at all. We are familiar with the imagined reasons for the change sometimes spoken of as established by Pliny's letter to be general at his time. Some say, the secrecy necessitated by persecution: others, the necessary hour for poor, especially slaves: others, the disorders exemplified at Corinth. But all these are pure conjectures, and besides they are reasons for what is not even professed to be proved to have been a fact.

The question of the change, and of reasons for it, appears long before the well-known letter of S. Augustine, on which the chief feeling on the subject rests. S. Cyprian, 150 years earlier, and himself the representative Ecclesiastical Father, accounts for the change by his well-known reply to Cacilius, 'Christ offered in the Evening, that the hour might set forth the decline and evening of the world ; but we celebrate the Resurrection of the Lord in the morning.' (Ep. 63 . 16.) If Fasting had been the reason and was an essential principle, S. Cyprian was not the man to omit it.

In regard to Eucharistic hours, apart from fasting, I must here notice an argument which was not before me when I wrote the main part of this discussion. A paper has been presented to me by advocates of Fasting Communion as the most satisfactory statement to represent their reasons. Its chief contribution to the discussion consists of an interesting set of three historical notices, by which the writer traces backward from the Middle Ages an alleged Church rule regulating the Eucharistic hour to be on Feasts at Early Morning, on Fasts in the Evening, on Half Fasts in the Afternoon. The writer's object is to shew that the hour of day was not a matter of concern to the Church, but only the rule of previous Fasting. I must say frankly that the paper appears to me to answer itself. It raises two questions : 1. To what date is the rule referred ?   2. Does it depend on Fasting ? Now if the rule is supposed to refer to Fasting, it can scarcely belong to the first ages. Half Fasts do not appear to have been primitive, but only late relaxations. The first fasts were, so far as we know, only the Jewish ' twice a week,' even Lent being a custom of very gradual growth. The first feasts were only Sunday, the Day of the Resurrection, and especially Easter Day, the chief Resurrection Feast : even Christmas being of later arrangement. Christians kept the Almanac of the Roman Civil year, like other people, only marking on it their Sundays, and other days as they grew : but the Dictionary of Christian Antiquities (Calendar) says that near the end of the Fifth Century a full Almanac only contained four feasts of Christ and six of martyrs. But the Almanac gave, of course, the Roman civil days as divided for regular national use into *Dies Fasti*, *Profesti*, and *Intercisi*, i.e., days of business, of no business, of half business. The Civil Law prescribed that Sacrifices and Recreations might begin on *Dies Fasti* in the evening, on *Profesti* as early as wished, on *Intercisi* when business was over. At first Christian worship would have had to follow the regular rule for all worship, and so could begin, as Pagans did, in early morning on *Dies Profesti*, in the afternoon on half-holidays, not till Evening on *Fasti*. But this was not by Church rule, nor in reference to fasting, but by civil law. In that sense variety of hours of worship must have been primitive, and it would have corresponded to the variety of Eucharistic hours, traced back in the paper before me as a Church rule, but which has no meaning as a Church rule at first. In later days the Church formed its own Almanac on the Civil one, and as She transformed Pagan buildings and festivals into Christian, She made Fasts, Feasts, and Half-holidays on the old division of Civil days. But rules for beginning worship on different kinds of days would have been already established, only not in reference to fasting, but as beginning each day at the earliest hour admissible by law on the particular day. Pliny's letter probably illustrates this. The Christian irregularity was that they held an antelucan Sacrament ' *stato die*,' which is usually taken to mean on Sundays, and probably does so, but which means at any rate ' on a fixed day of their own,' which was illegal. Sundays would cause their only irregularity, as the two weekly fasts, if the Eucharist was celebrated at all on them, would throw it into the evening, when it would be always legal. The Jews' Sabbath had been a preparation in the Roman world for Sunday. But apart from all this account of the probable origin of variety in Eucharistic hours, what does the Church rule, traced in the paper before me, itself say ? It says, That the hour varied on Feasts, Fasts, and Half Fasts. What is this but saying, that the Feasts, Fasts, and Half Fasts, were existing independently of the Eucharist, which had its rules made for it by those divisions of days ? So then the Fasts were not constructed for the sake of the Eucharist to be preparation for it, but the Fasts dominated the Eucharist by not allowing that to be celebrated during their time of continuance. The rule alleged might illustrate the importance attached to Fasts, as enough to dominate the Eucharist, but it is so far from illustrating, that it contradicts, any idea of the Eucharist requiring the Fast to precede as its preparation. The principle of the regulation is that the Eucharist should begin the day. The result (though not the origin) of it was that in all its varying hours (after the establishment of Church Days, in the place of Civil Days) it followed fasting. And this result seems to be interpreted to have been its intention, which (from the facts of the case) it could not have been. Such a connection does not appear before the fourth Century.

Very little therefore comes out of the interesting historical argument. S. Augustine's letter remains the chief proof of the supposed rule of fasting, and while the statement given above seems to do away with the generally supposed Church custom against Evening Communions, it really leaves the question just where it was in respect of the main subject of interest, Sunday Evening Communions. For Sunday the evidence remains unaltered, That in the New Testament the instances are all in the evening, and after the New Testament no instances of Evening Communion have been known till these last fifty years, besides the well known 'Exception that proves the rule' on Maundy Thursday. If the hours which the Church has established, are the best and truest, we are not bound to go back to the Evening, because Christ's last hours were in the Evening. So says S. Augustine. I think wisely. On the other hand, as S. Chrysostom says, Though we may protest that we have not taken on ourselves to break established custom in this, yet we shall shrink from calling 'sin,' still less 'mortal sin,' that, to call which sin, would be to condemn Christ Himself.

I have dwelt so long on this side of the question, because it is on these points that strong feeling has been created in the discussion of Evening Communions. I cannot myself think that Evening Communions stand or fall with Fasting Communion, nor even with proof of rule or custom, of which I have spoken. They depend chiefly on the practical question of their spiritual expediency ; of which one side is the balance of danger to devotion. the other side requiring evidence being their necessity, or convenience approaching necessity. I do not think it true, putting the

H

question of fasting aside, that Evening Communions are like Mid-day Communions in their circumstances. Evening services all differ from morning ones. The hour, the lights, the crowd, the meals just finished, the evening companionship, and the night outside darkness and assembling, all make the character of evening services excitement rather than solemnity. I do not doubt that it has become the chief hour of church-going. Then busy mothers, housewives, servants, and Sunday laborers, are able naturally to be free, and rest from labours, which do not cease on Sunday, and can go to Church with nothing on their mind. I see no reason to question what I am assured by men who joined in introducing the practice, though they have abandoned it, that their experience was, that their Evening Communions never failed in reverence, quiet, or devotion. Still they have given them up, and their judgment, therefore, is against them. They think the morning better, and the evening not necessary. My instincts make me think the former, my ignorance perplexes me about the latter. I cannot believe the miscellaneous evening circumstances into which I cannot go more particularly, to be the best for the strain of spiritual mysteries. Wesleyan revivals in an excitable people have formed a warning ere now against evening spiritual excitement. Even for the quiet and devout there are disturbing elements all round. The evening temper of the Corinthians is near us all in some form or other, and in spiritual as well as other feelings ' extremes are ready to meet,' and reaction is constantly at hand. Without supposing the slightest irreverence or disorder in what I do not question being devout Communions, I do not feel them the safest or the best. Whether they are necessary to avoid whole-sale excommunication of classes who cannot make themselves heard, and who may be only too ready to acquiesce in impossibilities, is the point of my doubt. I have often wondered how the classes who (practically) cannot attend morning services, have opportunities for Communion. Is it a real answer to say, ' Sunday hours in houses must be reorganized ? ' Is it a real answer to say, ' People can come if they choose, however dependent and however distant they are ? ' Is it a real answer to say, ' No additional Communicants are drawn, who don't come in the morning,' unless special efforts are addressed to the particular classes who cause the question to exist, to bring them and not discourage them ? Fairness of trial and judgment is hard to get, and reluctance (which I think wise) to bring people generally to Evening Communions, may sacrifice some helpless classes. This is my sole question. I understand the alternative to be very early celebrations, at 5 or 6 a.m. I love to hear of clergy going out to their work at the hours when their people do, and I believe it gains them sympathy with their reality. But when numbers of Communicants at very early hours on Christmas and Easter Day are presented as an answer, I wish to know if they do not represent special efforts for such single days. Do they not absorb all the Sunday vitality and make the rest of the day a protracted time of listlessness, if not idleness? Can they be frequent? or are two early Communions a year to be preferred to more frequent Communions at other hours? Can one man multiply early celebrations and do his other work all day? Experience as well as the reason of the thing shows that (except for the particular people suited by 8 a.m., *i.e.*, the clergy and well-to-do young people) the change of hours, from the service most generally attended to a separate early celebration, reduces ordinary people to the minimum frequency of communicating. I am quite aware that people will judge differently which is best, fasting or frequency. I learnt early to value the rule of regular Communions, and I think frequency. There is at least some reason to consider whether the old arrangements of the services were not the most suitable and also the most primitive. Our Church intended Mattins to precede the Holy Communion, and that Holy Communion should follow Mattins as a separate service. The practice of Winchester Cathedral till lately seems to have followed the intention in latter days best, when Mattins were at 8 and Holy Communion at 10. I read that this was the use of Southwell Minster. Celebrations before Mattins were an innovation at about the same date as celebrations after Evensong. When I was an Undergraduate, I was made aware that attendance at them verged on being penal. We who have enjoyed early celebrations ought to remember that others have objected to them as much as we to evening ones. At the time they were introduced neither formed a part of party controversy, nor do I think it a worthy view to make them a party question. I adhere to my instinctive opinion that our Sunday evening services are not the best times for the Holy Communion. And I am certainly moved by the results of the very careful examinations which have led those Bishops who began them to abandon them, not lightly, but on conviction of their not being the best. But all the people cannot have the best, I am afraid. And in parishes where earnest clergy have judged, simply from knowledge of their people, that there are classes of people excommunicated by rules of early and fasting Communion, I have made up my mind, from the time that I had to form a practical judgment on the question as

Bishop for this Diocese, that clergy must be trusted to balance the necessity and danger, and to employ the new method, if there is justifying occasion, with the same venture as we are ready to shew in what some people feel sensational mission revivals.

'Sacramental Confession.' If by this is meant, as I have gathered, that before communicating a person is bound always to make a private confession to a priest and receive private absolution, I cannot express too strongly my utter dissent from such a rule of compulsory private confession. I may be very ignorant, but I cannot understand how it can be compatible with any frequency of Communion. I own that I do not know practical details of working the system, but supposing the numbers returned as communicating on Easter Day were to be weekly, not to say daily, communicants at the early hours which would be necessary, I cannot imagine the feat of their ' being privately confessed.' If the object is to bring their absolution up to the moment of Communion, nothing else could even profess to satisfy this. Many things may happen in a night. Anything less complete seem to fail as much as an essential rule does if dispensation is admitted. Anything less ceases to claim discussion as Sacramental Confession, and to fall under the distinct and more general question of Compulsory Confession, or what is called the system of the Confessional.

The high motive with which such a system is advocated again; the amount of laxity requiring to be braced, which it is hoped to discipline by confession; the blessing which pious people so disposed have found in its practice; and the natural fitness of offering to all who need help and advice and comfort, opportunities for ' opening their grief ' : all these claim and have my full recognition. But they do not prevent my feeling and saying most strongly, that there is no one of the mediæval developments which I believe to be so deadly, both to priest and people, as the system included in the Confessional. I shall, however, only speak of its enfeebling character. A priest stands as spiritual doctor ; and a doctor's assurance to a patient that he is out of danger when his malady has reached that point, is not a more real or natural help to recovery, than the discreet spiritual doctor's assurance to a spiritual patient, that his repentance and amendment have reached forgiveness, and need be no more a burden. An awakened sinner may well seek such assurance before beginning to communicate. But to make it even ' a counsel of perfection,' that pious Christians should not draw near in faith without having a priest's permission, is an enfeebling valetudinarian system, only to be compared to healthy people being required to ask their doctor's leave to eat their breakfast. To make it a routine for all sorts and conditions of men, is a system about which I happily feel no call to speak. It is to me simply incredible. We must however remember that the aim of Sacramental confession professes to be Spiritual restoration, and so it represents a belief that Sacramental efficacy is not mechanical or material, but depends on the Spiritual condition of the recipient. In this respect it presents the same happy inconsistency with materialism as is presented by so many of the externals supposed to be associated with the Roman materialist theory.

'Ceremonial.' I pass, thirdly, to the separate points of ceremonial which have caused dispute. The three questions affecting them are, 1. Are they legally admissible either as old uses never abrogated, or as good additions not prohibited by omission of directions for them? On this question of legality I have said throughout that I am not intending now to speak at all. 2. Are they symbolic, *i.e.* used to teach particular doctrines or ideas, or are they æsthetic, *i.e.* used to stir worshippers through their senses? 3. If they are symbolic of doctrine, is the doctrine English or Roman? It will be simplest to take the last question first. Because none of the disputed points, The Eastward Position, Altar Lights, Vestments, Hymns, Incense, or even Ceremonial Ablutions, befit a Roman better than an English Sacramental doctrine. Neither symbolically nor æsthetically do they imply material more naturally than Spiritual Presence of Christ. I admit that revivers of the Ceremonial, when pressed not to disquiet people for trifles, have spoken darkly of their importance for 'the Doctrine,' but as they never said what doctrine, and repudiate any disloyal teaching, I suppose this to have been only a mystification to maintain the Ceremonial. That sense of mystification has discredited the Ceremonial: but that is not my point. My point is that the Ceremonial is more reasonably fitted to imply the English doctrine of Spiritual Presence than the Roman of material, and therefore, unless Roman doctrine be avowed, it need not be presumed, and if avowed, it should be dealt with in itself. Without ignoring the dark utterances to which I have referred, I am nevertheless convinced, that the lovers of Ceremonial have generally no idea of any but Spiritual worship in the Sacrament. That Spiritual worship is aided for them by these accessories. To them the Ceremonial is not Romish nor superstitious, but an uplifting help to true Spiritual worship, and it is clearer-sighted as well as larger-hearted to connect these aids with full and careful teaching of Spiritual Sacramental doctrine, than to condemn them as conveying erroneous doctrine, which does not naturally belong to them. In this respect it is that I regard words differently from Ceremonial. Ceremonial *may* be brought in as part of Romish system, but it need not be brought in for anything but its own use, and requires teaching to make it Romish : words must be brought in for their meaning. Ceremonial not only need not suit error better than truth, but it need not mean any teaching at all beside dignity in worship. Before Ceremonies can be called symbolic, the doctrine must first be established. A doctrine once established, it will be legitimate to illustrate it by parables from Ceremonial, or to create Ceremonial to illustrate it by parables. But ornaments may be turned by individual fancy to all manner of parables, and it cannot be supposed that individual fancy would therefore be entitled to interpret the Church to teach all that fancy's parables, because She uses the ornaments. The Church must interpret her emblems herself. Individuals have no right to state their own parables as Church doctrines. Flights of rhetorical fancy have been only too readily taken in all ages of the Church as matter-of-fact definite teaching about religious emblems. Symbolism may be a poetical language of Ceremonial, and poetry may be the vehicle of inexpressible truths, but it is mere arguing in a circle to imagine a particular meaning for an existing Ceremonial, and then say that the use of the Ceremonial proves that meaning to be recognized by the Church as true. Of course the difference presented above between words and Ceremonies is one only of degree. Ceremonies *may* be brought in because they are Romish, and with an ulterior object of arguing in a circle about them that their acceptance means the acceptance of Romish doctrine. I am aware that much of the objection to advances in ritual has risen from suspicion of such motives, and I do not say that there has been nothing to create that suspicion. But even so they have been introduced and accepted on the professed ground of their being beautiful and helpful in themselves. And I believe most people are prepared to consider them in themselves now, as æsthetic accessories simply, which may be judged as simply matters of feeling or taste. The form of worship has itself, of course, formed a marked difference between the two Churches, apart from doctrine. But English feeling may have changed about our form of worship without its thought changing in regard to our doctrine. That it has universally so changed is clearly not true. Dislike to much Ceremonial in itself exists in full strength, in some, maybe, simply from habit or ' Puritan prejudice,' but in very many from preference for simplicity over the distractions created by acts and accessories which seem trivial, or theatrical, or tedious. Older men feel that the quiet reverent company ' where hearts are of each other sure,' which has been their ideal of Christian Communion, is more precious to them than the music, the glitter, the paraphernalia, the crowd, the half-hearted non-communicants and children, substituted for that peaceful solemnity as the highest act of worship. But this is an age when parents must obey their children, and old people ought, no doubt, to be more independent of surroundings than young, and in matters of taste and feeling, if younger Churchmanship needs to be wakened more than soothed, by all means waken it. At any rate, accessories are matters of taste or feeling, not of doctrine or principle. Their degree ought to be regulated by fitness for each congregation. But before men condemn the development of accessories as superstitious, each should consider whether their own devotion never needs to be wakened, so that they can call it superstitious for others to wish for helps to waken theirs. I may myself like services as short and simple as may be, I may find Ceremonial distracting, and fear its becoming artificial and engrossing, and deprecate, therefore, its elaboration. Many are of this mind. They claim consideration from the clergy. But can we say that others who love richness of music, art, and ceremony must be less real or more super-stitious than ourselves ? When I think how devotion flags, even at the most solemn services, I cannot call it superstition to con-centrate devotion up to its fullest tension, at least for one central moment, by any aids which may stir people's senses as well as thought to waken them out of themselves to worship. That is the aim of Sacramental Ceremonial, and in that aim it is not symbolic, but æsthetic ; it is not doctrinal, but emotional ; it is not Romish, but human. The Spiritual Presence supposed by every act of worship is surely enough to make a real believer in it bow down even to the ground, without suspicion of disloyalty, superstition, idolatry. The more we insist on the Spiritual operation of the Sacrament on the soul, the more natural we make it to add to the act of worship every appeal available to stir the worshippers' spirit to its fullest activity and most impressionable self-surrender. Were it a material power in the Elements to which we looked to transmute the soul through the body, such material operation might dispense with Art and Ceremonial. Ceremonial is no doubt in one aspect the public expression of the joint homage of the whole body of worshippers to God ; but even therein it seems to carry each separate worshipper away to join that homage of Praise to the Spiritual Presence which is the centre of all worship, and in that self-surrender to Communion with Him. Spirit seeks the operation of Spirit in the Sacrament. Surely, and even therefore, the human Spirit—compounded as it is of divers parts, not only of reason, memory, and thought, but of sensations also, which so enwrap our attention—finds help in stirring accessories of Ceremonial.

I will now touch the several points disputed.

'Eastward Position.' When I supposed that the natural meaning of a Rubric's words was the only point to determine, I came to the opinion (that the Table being shaped and placed as it is, and end not being side) the only question answered exactly by the Rubric's direction was, Is the Priest to begin by standing at the centre, or the north side ? And though very ready to stand at the north end, when so ordered, I judged myself the literal phrase to be more exactly satisfied by standing at the north front corner. But I am lapsing into legal questions, and will pass on. The change from north end to west side is the most observable of the changes, and it may be used most perversely to contradict the spirit of our service, if the Priest is led to imitate Romish practice in making acts or prayers secret. But in itself, it is Congregational rather than Sacerdotal, according to the reply of the Bishops to the Puritans, that ' For what is addressed to the people, it is fit to turn towards them, but for joining with them in prayer, to turn with them.' In this respect it is like the adoption of surpliced choirs, processional entrances met by Congregational rising, a choir-seat instead of reading-desk for the Minister, and other unifications of Minister with people, instead of the Parson's separate dress entrance and position. It has sometimes been wondered that people anxious to emphasize the Consecration did not welcome the judgment that the Consecration should be marked by the Priest moving then to the front from the north end. Mechanical retort wonders that people who were not anxious for that, did not welcome the permanent eastward position which diminished that emphasis. For the Consecration I cannot question that the natural position is at the front centre, and that the process of carrying the vessels round to the north end is needless clumsiness. For the earlier part of the service, the north end may reasonably have been adopted that the minister might see the people and be heard by them. It would represent the principle of our Church that the Services ought to be ' understanded of the people.'

The fitness of the eastward position does not extend to ' what is addressed to the people,' whether Scripture, Exhortations, Sermon, or Notices. But as a fact it does not usually impede the people's hearing, but only the Minister's seeing. Nor does it make any difficulty about ' the manual acts ' being seen. If men brood over the elements on their elbows as for some secret performance, that is a wilful violation of the Rubric, but it is difficult to see how such an undignified attitude can be called Sacrificial or Sacerdotal. In the middle ages it was called Necromantic.

'Altar and altarwise position.' When or why western churches adopted the table-shape and east wall place, is an unsolved problem. They were not primitive, nor are they Eastern Christian, any more than they were Jewish, Greek, Roman, or Egyptian. An altar is an altar from its use, not its position. Our usual present position suits churches built to it, and forms a chief centre to unite worship. But in many of our deep chancels, the primitive place at the arc of the presbytery would serve as well : and still better the place, used in some foreign churches, at the east of the nave. Disengagement from the east wall does not make a table, nor east wall place an altar. A tablewise position might be made by setting seats round and making Communicants sit round ; but all the rubrics of our service contradict that usage. As contrast to that, any arrangement which supposes worship and kneeling may be called altarwise. But whether Altar, as the place for sacrifice, is English or Romish, is simply the question what sacrifice is meant. This we have discussed before. As a place for slaying a victim, it is not primitive or English, whether it be Romish or not. As a place for presenting offerings, it is primitive and may well be English, though our Liturgy does not employ it. Wherever and in the same sense as sacrifice is retained in our Liturgy, altar is its correlative. But ' The Lord's Table ' scarcely differs from Altar. It does not imply a social meal of men, but the Lord's Feast offered to God in His Memorial, from which His sacred food is ministered to His servants, kneeling in sacred obeisance at reverent distance. So regarded, Table and Altar are the same. Still it is true that altar is more entirely a word of religion, and supposing of course its meaning to be rightly defined by true teaching about our sacrifice, the satisfaction of its greater solemnity involves no superstition. Our Church uses the word in one of her services. Our Lord directs His disciples to bring their gifts to the Altar. Though ' Table ' is a name in use in the early writers, Altar is the name of most natural and common use. Its revival among us is too general to bear any special controversial meaning, and marks only a sense of sacred dignity.

'Altar Lights.' The Symbolism attributed to these could not be called Romish at any rate, but really it seems disabled by diversity of interpretation, *e.g.*, the Divine and human nature of Christ, the Word and the Spirit, the Old and New Testament, &c. Two lights may symbolize any pair of illuminating powers : but without authoritative interpretation they symbolize none in particular. They give a feeling of life. Flame has been felt in all religions the most immaterial symbol of living unearthly power and purity. One central unextinguished light, like that of Vesta, might be more fitting than the pair of candles which have to be unnaturally gigantic not to look like furniture. So in Roman Churches a constant lamp makes them feel alive. Only then its symbolism of a living presence is contradicted by the other more special Romish symbol to which it is attached. So our 'Altar Lights' would be contradictory symbols of Christ's presence at the time when Sacramental symbols are presenting Him otherwise. But no meaning can be attached to them which would make them imply Romish more than English doctrine. At first they were lighted at the Gospel, to signify The Light of the World. Feeble as they are in broad daylight, they suggest disparaging questions. If they were adduced as evidential survivals of very Early Celebrations, they might consistently be disused at hours when forced meanings have to be invented to account for lights. 'Altar Candlesticks' stood not only in cathedrals and colleges when I was a boy, but in very un-Romish churches, before early celebrations were revived or evening Communions invented. The candles were not lighted. So little did the churchwardens value their lighting power, that when evening services were begun in our parish church, a very un-Romish old lady had to provide wax candles that it might not be the only dark place. Possibly churchwardens would not now keep lights burning through the week, at least in churches where people do not resort. But to many people an everburning light would be a simple and meaning symbol, fitted for all times when more specially Christian symbols are not presenting more special teaching. Candles lighted ceremonially during the service belong, of course, to a distinct subject, already discussed, as sensational dramatic accessories.

'Vestments.' The ritual of special vestments for the Sacrament and the ritual of a black gown for preaching need not now be discussed. Special dress for marriages, funerals, sacraments, and seasons has much to say for itself. So has the unchanging ministry presenting itself the same in all its offices. I was glad when the black gown was simplified away even from sermons which were not so clearly parts of the service as those in the Communion service. I am well pleased that my official scarf does not change colour. But when I wear my Cathedral cope, as the Canons bid me, I feel no change of doctrine induced in me by it. Even a richer one would not make me contradict the Prayerbook. Chasubles are still *Sub judice*, but as regards Symbolism, if Chasubles are called 'Sacrificial' (which I think a very unhistoric account of their origin), that only brings up again the twice discussed question, about the meanings of Sacrifice. But when vestments are said to be essential for 'doctrine,' I wonder what the doctrine can be, which was not able to be held (say) by Keble or Pusey, who were certainly not Vestiarians. Rich dresses are things in themselves. As I said in my last Charge, travellers liked their unaccustomed gorgeousness and wanted to have at home what they admired abroad. It was not as symbolising doctrine, but as more beautiful, that those who liked these liked them, and the objections about them have rested on preference for simplicity over magnificence. No doubt taste for the former has been called Puritan, taste for the latter Popish, but people are now generally prepared to judge them on their merits apart from either prejudice. For it is prejudice alike to say, Vestments shew false teaching, or Teaching depends on Vestments. Vestments are of all things matter for each Church to regulate, and in each Church its regulations need not prescribe uniformity. In cathedrals, parish churches, private chapels, such accessories may fitly differ in proportion. Rules for parish churches must respect the old maxim, '*Sectetur partem conclusio doteriorem*,' and not prescribe impossibilities for the poor. But that would not be a sensible limitation on private chapels, where taste and cost are no public concern.

'Music.' No Symbolism is attached to music simply. The general question of its use as an accessory has been enough discussed. It is the accessory which by common consent may most reasonably be used sometimes and omitted at others. Our special sacrifice of praise and thanksgiving is as such a service for music. Our special Communion Service is more peaceful without, for people who wish to pray : though hymns during times of waiting may help those who have no thoughts of their own. To protract early celebrations with tedious music at unmusical hours keeps people away. Music, beautiful at S. Paul's, is distressing in a midland village. But these are all questions of feeling or expediency. Music belongs to praise if to anything. In regard to music at The Sacrament, the objections have been to particular hymns, and on the ground that they imply Romish doctrine. I have been unable to see that the Agnus Dei is more Romish at one time in the service than at another, and if any hymn is fitting for the moment when worshippers are dwelling specially on Christ's atonement, it is that. A Spiritual Presence is more fitted to be saluted with the hymns, ' Blessed is He that cometh in the name of the Lord,' and ' O Lamb of God, that taketh away the sins of the world,' than any imagination of a material presence of which such words could only be imperfectly true in a lower sense. The Benedictus has indeed disappeared from our Communion service, but all the other music, composed by the great masters for the Roman Mass, are settings for words forming parts of our service, and their music has no Romishness about it, nor are lovers of their music more Romish for being so. The music is the music.

' Incense.' This is probably to most English people the most foreign accessory, and it has probably been most advocated for Symbolism. But I think that really it is of all the one most a matter of taste. It will scarcely represent to many the presence of the Holy Spirit, which is its interpretation, except when it is said to present the upfloating of prayers, because in the Revelation the incense of heaven is said to be the prayers of saints. Either meaning is, however, at any rate apart from Roman controversy. Nothing could fall more completely under the general question of more or less accessories. It may be to some an uplifting sensuous accessory, to others an unmeaning distraction or even a distasteful annoyance. I have no taste for it, but if it is to be used, I must say that I have no sympathy with the special limitation imposed on its use. New light may perhaps rank it with other accessories in this. Its foreignness is its objection, and though our chilly, dark climate might seem to make it just the accessory for our churches, it feels to me to befit better the finer southern atmospheres where it does not hang heavy like a fog. A graver, æsthetic doubt about its fitness for us lies in its performance. The more subtle the accessory the finer must be its exhibition. Soundless southern movements and sentimental southern faces in natural accord with Ceremonial seem to belong to the dreamy influence of incense. Rough, honest Englishmen and shy awkward English boys swing censers with less fascinating artlessness than supple southern acolytes with southern quickness formed by heredity and drill to perfect artistic simplicity. I have been censed by even a trained English curate, but the force and enjoyment of his thoroughness were not ethereal, nor its unexpected influence uplifting. However, if the drill is worth the time, incense is only one more sensuous accessory of movement, cloud, and fragrance, occupying people's senses with effects which grow to be associated with church and worship. It is neither sacred nor heretical, but a matter of taste.

In the remaining small point of minor gestures, such as crossings, genuflections, elevations, prostrations, the question is not so clear. For crossings, bowings, turnings, genuflections, the regulating principle seems to be their reality and adequate dignity, and that will set limits to frequency and demonstrativeness, so as to avoid as far as possible the impression or the feeling of rule, routine formality, and attitudinising. For example, To bow in obeisance to the Divine Presence on entering and leaving Church, is only what belief in that Presence suggests naturally to all who would shew such respect to human dignity or friend. But perpetual repetitions are as much out of place in one case as the other. To turn to the East at the recital of Creeds is one of the oldest Church forms of special profession, which is liable to be weakened by frequent repetitions at other points of the service. But the personal reality of reverence in leader and teacher will be the conditioning element of reality to all enlisted in a system of such minor acts. That they help devotion as constant reminders is clearly very often true ; that they may be formal fidgets hard to maintain with meaning is no less often true. Their fitness is marred by multiplication, which tends to lower them to triviality from solemnity. But it is rare now to see excess in such demonstrativeness, and the reduction of trivial mannerisms in the present decade encourages the assurance that nothing sickly or theatrical survives long. When made parts of ministerial ceremonial, I cannot speak of them so simply. Sometimes they seem to contradict the solemn unity of greater acts, by being made petty and distracting adjuncts to them ; as in Benediction, the sign of the Cross brings in a second contrary idea, which, if of constant truth, has no fitness for acts of special character. Still this scarcely needs observation. I cannot say this of some elevations and prostrations. No impulsive uplifting can be too high for offerings to God, no obeisance too low for the great mercies of God, of which the Sacrament is memorial. Prostration is more reasonable for a believer, than to sit unmoved from mere fear of soiling dress or trouser. But it is not in transport of impulsive worship that the paten is lifted, not in the manner of offering, but in the manner of exhibition, with ingenious devices to present a wafer over the Priest's head to the people behind ; and if a Priest takes on himself at the moment of such artificial elevation to interpolate into a service, to every minute point in which importance is attached, Behold the Lamb of God ; and if after such special act and words he prostrates himself ; he cannot expect ordinary comprehension to discriminate that particular combination of acts and words from the ' Idolatry to be abhorred of all faithful Christians,' which is so clearly, in the last Rubric of our Communion Service, declared not to be taught or countenanced in that service. Ceremonial accessories and even hymns stand in varying degrees outside of the office : but if a Priest presumes to omit sentences, because he does not like them, or introduce sentences to emphasize his particular views, his fault is the more serious from the importance attached by him to the alterations and the importance which he knows to be attached to the service.

'The mixed Chalice.' This seems made a question of archæology, not of doctrine : to be revived, not for Symbolism, but for unity with primitive and general practice. Few could think of mixing wine and water as a symbol of the union of Priest and people. I do not know that any one disputes that the Cup must have been mixed at the Paschal Institution. In the Mediterranean regions of primitive Christianity wine was not drunk at meals without water : Unmixed wine was called ' Sheer,' and to drink it was what drinking raw spirits is with us. That the Sacramental Chalice under special circumstances was diluted to an extreme degree, sufficing to meet total abstainers' difficulties, we learn from S. Cyprian. But the argument from this to ourselves rests on the disputable premiss, that we are bound to have the same Cup as that of the Institution, which might as well require the wine to come from Palestine. A Ceremonial drop of water in the wine is not the original Cup, of half wine half water. And if that Cup was diluted, not for any Ceremonial Symbolism, but (which is the only basis of assuming that it was diluted at all) only because it was the way of drinking customary in the country at the time, it would seem that it gave us the example of using the Cup customary in each country. In England it has been often, and even judicially, thought a cheat to water the wine, and the best and richest wine has been the rule for provision. Such an idea seems as honorable as that of uniformity with countries of different habits. It is an abuse of language to speak of an unmixed Cup separating us from Catholic Christendom ; as it would be to say that, because at the feast of unleavened bread the bread at the Institution was unleavened, therefore the Sacramental bread must always be unleavened, or because the Institution was in an Upper Chamber, the Sacrament must always be in an Upper Chamber, or because there were twelve Apostles there must always be. All which things have been said by different people. I only observe further : 1. That the disuse of water is an alteration distinctly made in our service ; 2. That if the Cup is mixed, it seems more worthy to do it openly : 3. That if customs have varied as to the time and place of mixing, even custom leaves that open ; 4. That the unmixed Cup is what the Rubric directs.

'Ceremonial Ablutions.' On the last of the ritual points I shall

be thought, perhaps, unreasonable myself in having personal feeling
about a point which has now been judged to be outside of all consideration. The name had seemed to me to imply that they were
regarded as Ceremonial, and the elaborateness of gradation prescribed
for their execution has baffled my attainment. Why unconsecrated
wine should be subject for so much more precise order than consecrated, I have not been instructed, nor how, after the most scrupulous
execution, the object can be secured that no infinitesimal solution of
the consecrated wine should remain to be absorbed by the final
abstertion. But these questions have not exercised me, so much as
what seems to me (strangely, perhaps, but very decidedly) to be the
inconsistent irreverence of cleansing the vessels upon the place
which those who advocate the practice exalt to the highest sacredness. Be it Table, or be it Altar, how is the place of Sacred Feast,
still more if it is the place of Sacrifice, the place for cleansing
vessels ? I desire that all things be done decently and in order : I
would not call scrupulosity superstitious : I see the matter left for
reverent discretion : but Rabbinical minuteness has no dignity, and
the method of Ceremonial ablutions seems to me to frustrate its
purpose of reverence. I do not myself undertake them. Where
they are wished, I leave them to the clergy responsible. They
offend my sense of fitness, however unreasonably.

If I am expected to say what I should myself direct for this
necessary work, which is judged to be no part of the service, and
for which no directions have been thought necessary by our Church,
I am content, so far as reverence is concerned, that the vessels be
cleansed at the Credence Table. But I prefer that, the service
ended, no state of slovenly disorder be thought fit in Church, but
that the vessels be left ' covered with a fair linen cloth ' either in
their place or on the Credence Table, while the people go away, and
afterwards one of the clergy should return for the vessels and cleanse
them at the Piscina, if there be one, or in the Vestry or Sacristy. I
do not mean that cleansing the vessels is a priestly office, or that
laymen are not holy enough for that. But I gladly welcome the
clergy's reverent care.

These are the thoughts which I have for some time prepared to
lay before the Diocese on these disputed points of ritual. I hope
that they may come as ghosts flitting over deserted battle-fields,
shadows of judgments which might have interested when they were
suppressed. I have spoken untechnically, and left law and the
courts alone. Not that I think that no one regards them, for I
believe that much of the past distress has been only caused by
doubts if things might legally be done ; and now that new light
has shewn old mistakes, such people will feel happily relieved of a

responsibility. But that has not been my particular object, but rather to use this opportunity of my Visitation to publish my opinions on questions, which I have been asked during these years, when circumstances imposed reserve at the time, but which I feel it due to the Diocese and also to myself to take the first proper opportunity of answering publicly.

May I say, that what has struck me most repeatedly in these discussions is, that the objections raised on the points insisted on by what I must venture to call different schools in the Church, have been just the opposite to what I should myself have expected their principles, as generally understood, to suggest ? This has often encouraged me to hope that fresh consideration of such points may so shift their aspects as to extend greatly the range of agreement, and also to reduce differences from the level of principles to the level of personal preferences.

Some of the questions have come into the public arena since I was engaged on this publication, but I have scarcely had occasion to add anything in consequence.

Some considerations on particular points in the Communion Service I have omitted, because a very able and complete treatment of the Communion Service has been published by the Bishop of Salisbury as his Visitation Charge for 1891, which I commend to my brethren, and which I feel it superfluous to repeat.

As I began, so I will end, by saying, that in the Midlands it is rare for questions about Eucharistic doctrine and methods to be raised. It does not follow that when they rise they are not acute, or that I have not had occasion to reflect on them. But I do not think that cases are more than singular, where the people have cause to complain of want of considerateness on the part of their clergy. Nor do I find that if a clergyman is a man of zeal and sympathy with his people, and is respected for his character and sense of duty, there is much disposition on the part of the people to quarrel with his methods even if they are not what would be chosen by them. Varieties of method affect town parishes comparatively little, now that our town churches interchange parishioners so freely. In villages adherence to the methods of the Prayerbook is of the gravest consequence, both as the *via media* in which all may unite, and as what villagers can feel comes to them with full authority. What they expect and have a right to expect is loyalty to the Church of England as represented to them by the Prayerbook. Loyalty to the Church of England as her ministers and human sympathy with English people as brothers, are the two things needful in clergy for trust and regard. To believe in the Church of England and in the English people is an English clergyman's earthly wisdom and strength. No other church combines the excellencies of the Church of England for the free sober thoughtful independent Godfearing people of England, whose religious reverence has been formed on the Bible and by the Sunday. Other nations may have formed theirs on other bases. That does not so much concern us. *Spartam nactus es, hanc orna.* English people are our people, it is for them English clergy have to live and think and work and pray. The primitive way of being Catholic was to be National, and that is, and let us hope will long continue, our English way. The Bidding Prayer calls on us to Pray for Christ's Holy Catholic Church, especially that pure and Apostolic Branch of it established in this realm. But we need not care to assert that by adding an epithet to its name of Church of England, any more than we need state its history as being, not a Church which joined simply, like German princes, in protest against Roman errors, but a Church which reformed them. It need not call itself Catholic or call itself Reformed, but simply the Church of England. Its standard is the Prayerbook. Laxity of custom seems to condone neglect which falls short of our Prayerbook's directions, but such neglect is as lawless as excess beyond them, and it furnishes a natural justification *ad hominem* against complaints of excess. The Prayerbook is the rule which the clergy have promised to follow, and whatever can be shewn to be ordered in it will be accepted by the people. It is a noble inheritance with which the clergy and the people will be wise to be content, and to unite in developing the robust Churchmanship contained in its principles. The young and earnest require some subject of contention, in which they shall be better than their fathers. May they seek it where it is to be found, in the spiritual war with sin and misery and ignorance and discord, which fills the social life of our crowded and struggling population! May they as true sons of the Church of England see and keep the true law of proportion, in which specially our Church seeks to follow the Gospel! May they contend for the weightier matters of the Law Justice Mercy and Truth, and their Ceremonial will be real and reverent. *Præcipuè in Christi pace permaneant.*

PRINTED BY J. WHITTINGHAM, SOUTHWELL.

www.ingramcontent.com/pod-product-compliance
Lightning Source LLC
Chambersburg PA
CBHW030717110426
42739CB00030B/703